New Concepts In Dehydrated Food Cookery

New Concepts In Dehydrated Food Cookery

Hundreds of New Ideas and Tested Recipes for Enjoying Home Dehydrated Foods

Barbara Densley

International Standard Book Number
0-88290-126-5

Library of Congress Catalog Card Number
79-89357

Horizon Publishers Catalog and Order Number
4021

Printed and Distributed in the
United States of America
by

**Horizon
Publishers &
Distributors**

**P.O. Box 490
50 South 500 West
Bountiful, Utah 84010**

In memory of

Clara Rozilla Maynard

July 7, 1886 - August 27, 1981

who devoted her life

to her posterity.

Acknowledgments

I wish to thank my parents for giving me an inquiring mind and a determination to keep working until I achieve my goals.

When I am in search of a recipe, our kitchen looks like the aftermath of a mini tornado. I owe my husband a great debt of gratitude for his help in cleaning up the debris.

After six more years of experimenting, even though I have had some failures, I am even more enthusiastic about dehydration as a choice method of preserving food. It is nutritious, convenient, has the advantage of less storage space, is a money saver, and it is just fun to do it!

I wish to thank our children and grandchildren for their support and encouragement to continue experimenting. To watch children's sparkling eyes light up as they watch hard potatoes soften as they reconstitute, and to hear their exclamations as they see the crisp golden chips come from the deep-fat fryer, is a joyous experience. To see how intrigued they are when a flat piece of orange leather made from the jack-o-lantern is reconstituted into a yummy pumpkin pie, or dehydrated strawberries are used to make delicious homemade ice cream—this is what dehydration is all about.

I would like to thank Reid Shelly for talking with me and sharing test results from his research project. I would also like to thank Dr. Clayton S. Huber, with the Food Science and Nutrition Department of Brigham Young University, for taking time to consult with me and for the information he supplied with regard to nutrient loss in dehydrated foods.

A special thank you to all of the people who encourage me and help me test recipes; and especially for their willingness to try my suggestions and then report back with the results.

As this book goes to press, the following people will give a big sigh of relief: the home economists from the Sacramento Municipal Utilities District; Katherine Kitchen, a food editor from the Sacramento Bee, the home economists from the Sacramento County Extension Service, USDA; and the Food Science Department at the University of California, Davis. I would like to thank them for their assistance to me in sharing their knowledge, answering my questions, and their patience with me.

And last but not least, a thank you to my publisher, Duane S. Crowther, president of Horizon Publishers and Distributors, who encourages me to write and then with forbearance, waits.

Contents

PART II

Introduction

We as a nation have a problem with obesity caused by too many empty calories and not enough exercise. We are plagued with diseases caused by obesity—high blood pressure, diabetes, hardening of the arteries, etc.

It is time to contemplate what we are doing wrong. Health and well being are directly related to nutrition. All nutrients work as a team in the body. Each individual's food needs vary depending on age, sex, physical size, illness and activity. To assure a well-balanced diet, people should eat a wide variety of foods daily.

When fresh foods are available, they, of course, are the most nutritious and desirable. Care must be taken with fresh foods to maintain their nutrition by harvesting, storing and cooking them properly.

Because very few plants are continuous producers, fresh foods are not always available. When surplus food is preserved by dehydrating, canning, or freezing, there is a loss of nutrients because of exposure to heat, light, air and the liquid used in each specific preservation method. It is necessary to choose wisely the method of preservation. Will the food's appearance, flavor and quality be such that it will be appetizing after it is preserved? Will it provide the nutritional value required for a healthy body?

Nature provided the first method of preservation: sun drying of grains and legumes. So that they could save some of their excess food, people observed nature and copied sun drying. They dried and stored meat, herbs, seeds and fruits for use when they were unavailable because they were "out of season."

Dehydration, because of its storage capabilities, has continued to improve and progress. Commercial companies started using solar energy for drying grapes, apples, figs, prunes and apricots; but because of the unreliability of the sun they are turning to controlled equipment to insure sufficient supply of product to meet the demand.

Because sun power is not available continually, solar dehydrators have not been too successful in producing a satisfactory product. With the proper combination of choice food, proper pretreatment, and an efficient electric dehydrator, it is possible to produce quality dehydrated products.

A new health awareness spreading across the country has created many enthusiastic persons who want to get back to nature. There has been an increase in home vegetable gardens with a desire to put some of the surplus food into storage for use "out of season." Many small fruit and vegetable stands have appeared on vacant lots, selling quantities of fresh fruits and vegetables for home processing.

Inflation has made food prices soar. Because of inflation it is imperative that each food dollar be spent wisely and that the food purchased be handled properly to get the most nutrition possible. The old addage by which I was raised, "Waste not, want not," is an important precept. Don't waste the surplus produce from the family garden—preserve it. While peoples of the world are starving, people in the United States are wasting food. Prepare your own foods instead of paying for costly processing, and avoid "junk" foods. Buy during the peak of the season and put some away as a low-cost budget stretcher for use at a later time.

When I first started with dehydration, very few people had heard of electric dehydrators for home use. Now they are available in department stores, health food stores, mail order catalogs, hardware stores, and specialty shops all over the country.

Six years have slipped by since the publication of my first book, *The ABC's of Home Food Dehydration*. While the basics of dehydration remain the same, I have learned some new methods for faster preparation which result in a finished product with a higher nutritional value.

Many people have said to me, "I have dried it, now what do I do with it?" In answer to that question comes this book, *New Concepts in Dehydrated Food Cookery.* I have learned some new techniques in preparing, dehydrating, and using dehydrated foods. These new concepts produce a quality food with a high nutritional value. Utilizing dehydrated foods, the recipes in this book have been developed for easy preparation at a low cost.

If you believe a recipe calls for too much of one kind of spice or seasoning, or not enough, change it. It is always possible to add, omit or substitute an ingredient. To omit olive oil and substitute a less expensive oil may change the flavor but the different taste may be more appealing. If you don't like onion, omit it. If a recipe calls for dehydrated herbs and you have a window herb garden, substitute fresh herbs (but remember to increase the amount). Be careful with amounts of liquid used in reconstitution and note changes required for high altitude cooking.

The 325 recipes have been arranged primarily in alphabetical order by the principal ingredient rather than in sections, such as desserts, main dishes or appetizers. This alphabetical order has been violated where a recipe calls for a sub-ingredient produced by another recipe. In these cases, for convenience in preparation of that dish, the sauce, filling, etc., follows immediately, even though it usually is not in alphabetical order.

The reader will find the index to be very helpful. It has been prepared as a cross reference. For an example, you may wish to use apricots in a meal. Looking under apricots in the index you will find main course, dessert, appetizers, snacks, etc. If you were to go to snacks or appetizers you would again find the same recipes. Therefore, if you are looking for any type of dish for a specific fruit or vegetable, look it up by name in the index. If you are looking for a particular type of dish, such as dessert, turn directly to desserts in the index and identify one that seems to fit the occasion. Each recipe is numbered. The number listed in the index refers to recipe numbers, not to page numbers.

In addition to recipes using dehydrated foods, this book contains general instructions pertaining to specific techniques and products. These instructions are placed throughout the book at the most appropriate location and may be found by the use of the index.

The chapter on "New Concepts" will share the knowledge I have gained through study and continued experimentation in searching for new, easier, and nutritionally better methods of preserving food by dehydration and reconstituting it satisfactorily.

PART 1

Tray of dehydrated foods

Hiker's Snack *Fruit leathers*

Kenny's Corn Pudding (#85)
Escalloped Potatoes

NEW CONCEPTS

1

What's New In Theory

Fresh fruits and vegetables, when harvested, continue to undergo chemical changes which can cause deterioration and spoilage of the food.

Water makes up over 90 percent of the weight of most fruits and vegetables. Cell walls give support, structure and texture to the fruit or vegetable. Water and other chemical substances are held within the cell walls.

Enzymes cause the loss of color, nutrients, flavor and texture of foods. These chemical compounds must be deactivated to protect the food. Blanching will deactivate the enzymes in vegetables. Blanching is the exposure of vegetables to boiling water, steam or microwave pretreatment for a brief period to stop the enzyme action and to help destroy microorganisms on the surface of vegetables.

The enzymes in fruits that cause browning and loss of vitamin C are controlled by using ascorbic and citric acid or sodium bisulfite.

Oxygen causes a chemical change that gives the food a rancid flavor. This problem is solved by using packaging that does not permit oxygen to get into the food.

All methods of food preservation change the texture of the food being preserved.

Canning changes the texture of fruits and vegetables. The textural change is not as apparent in foods that are cooked before eating because cooking also softens the cell walls. The changes are also less noticeable in starchy vegetables such as peas and corn.

With frozen food preservation, the water expands when it is frozen and the ice crystals cause the cell walls to rupture. When the produce is thawed it is softer than when it was raw. That is why it is suggested that frozen fruits be consumed before they have completely thawed.

Freeze-drying is a commercial process where the selected foods are frozen, placed in a near vacuum and heated, causing the ice to vaporize. As the crystals are removed it leaves the food's cell structure in tact which requires special handling to prevent crushing. Freeze-dried foods are more bulky to store and must be handled with care so as not to crush them. This process retains more nutritional value because of the speed in processing. The food also rehydrates more rapidly and, if it has not been crushed, it reconstitutes more nearly to the fresh size. It has a long storage life. Because of the high cost of processing, it is expensive.

Commercially dehydrated foods are prepared at such a constant dry heat that the moisture is reduced to 2 to 3 percent. The food is very compact and brittle. Most commercially dehydrated products are packed in vacuum and/or nitrogen-sealed cans, and have a long shelf life if left un-opened. Dry milk, eggs, or any product with milk or eggs in it has a shorter life than other dehydrated products. Dehydrated food is not as expensive as freeze-dried food.

Home dehydrated food is the least expensive of all methods of food preservation. People who grow their own fruits and vegetables can dehydrate the excess and help combat inflation. Now, science and modern technology have been applied to the age-old process with good results. Preserving food by dehydration is safe, practical, economical and nutritious. By harvesting the food when it is mature, processing it rapidly and storing it properly, there is no reason to not have maximum nutritional value.

Home dehydrated foods have a shelf life of one year for best nutritional value. If they are vacuum sealed and placed in a freezer they can be kept longer, but is there a need for more than a shelf life of one year? Season to season is a good guide line.

2

What's New In Dehydration Equipment

In the last six years, dehydration has come a long way with regard to equipment. There are still many companies marketing dehydrators, even though many others have gone out of business. The two major companies manufacturing electric dehydrators are Alternative Pioneering Systems (manufacturing the *Harvest Maid)* and Orton Enterprises International (manufacturing the *Excalibur Dehydrator).* Some of the important things to look for in a dehydrator are:

1. A fan and a heating element permitting a balance of air flow and heating capacity. If the fan capacity is too high for the element wattage, it may not be possible to maintain an adequate dehydration temperature within the dehydrator. Inadequate air movement will reduce drying speed, while too much air movement will cause unnecessary heat loss and a waste of energy.
2. An adjustable thermostat with up-front controls.
3. Check to see if the cabinet has any insulating qualities to help hold the heat inside the cabinet and dry the food rather than to heat up the air in the house.
4. High-limit protection to shut off the electricity to the unit should the temperature rise above a safe level because of a malfunction. The unit should also be UL listed and approved for safety measures.
5. It is convenient to use a dehydrator in the kitchen in the cold months of the year, so it is important to check the noise level of the unit to decide if it is acceptable for use in the house.
6. The weight of a unit is very important if the unit has to be moved often.
7. A filter is a nice feature for anyone drying food outside. It also prevents lint from getting into the dehydrator from the

air inside the home. This is an important feature for decoupage or photography projects dried in the dehydrator.

8. A recirculation adjustment on a dehydrator helps save energy and improve the product. In the recirculation mode, a portion of the cold air from outside is blocked and the warm air in the dehydrator is recirculated, thereby cutting down the cost of heating the cold air. This is good only when drying a full load of one food; otherwise, flavor transfer could be a problem. Two-thirds of the way through the drying cycle, if the vent is closed, the warm air recirculates across the food with just enough moisture to keep the outside of the food from getting crisp while the moisture in the center of the food is pulled to the outside and evaporated. This prevents case hardening and gives a softer end product. If the dehydrator is placed on recirculation before sufficient moisture has been removed, it can prolong the drying time of the food.

9. The capacity is important. When purchasing food in large quantities, it is necessary to have a dehydrator that will accommodate the food. When purchasing food in smaller quantities, it isn't necessary to have a large dehydrator. Many people have a large dehydrator that is used outside during the peak of the drying season and also have a small unit to use in the house during the winter months to make granola, yogurt rolls, leathers, dry bananas, etc.

10. Drying trays should be made of screening to let air circulate throughout the food. The ideal tray is one that is sturdy enough to not sag under the weight of the fresh produce being dried. Food-grade plastic screening that lifts off from the tray for ease in removing the food is the most desirable. Ease of cleaning is also an added feature. Rescreening can be a problem with trays that have metal frames where the screening is stretched and held into a groove with a rubber beading.

Solar Dehydrators

Because of high energy costs, solar dehydration is beginning to come forth. There are plans available to build direct, modified direct and indirect dehydrators.

Direct solar drying involves placing the food into direct sunlight. Indirect drying uses the sun's energy to heat air and then circulate it over the food without exposing the food to direct sunlight. Modified direct drying uses a glass to protect the food from the sun's ultraviolet rays. Solar dehydration is in its infancy. With time and experimentation, efficient solar dehydrators will emerge, providing quality dehydrated food with less expense.

In the tests conducted at Brigham Young University, the indirect solar dryer appeared to have the best potential. The direct dryer was least desirable because of high vitamin losses.

Microwave Dehydration

Some things can be dried in the microwave oven. However, true drying of fruits and vegetables is simply a physical change removing water and maintaining the food's cell structure. When the food is actually cooked, even when the oven is set at the lowest setting, the cell structure in going from raw to dry is chemically changed and altered.

With my experimentation in the microwave, I found that fruits with their high sugar content were susceptible to burning before sufficient moisture was removed from them to finish drying by standing overnight. The grated coconut molded after a week.

Vegetables, because of the required pretreatment by steaming, were dehydrated more successfully. When I removed the carrots from the microwave I did not believe they would be dry after standing overnight, but to my surprise they were dry the following morning.

Dehydrated fruits have a distinct flavor when they are dried which is not achieved when drying in the microwave because of the high temperature. This is a disadvantage in using the microwave. The space available in a microwave is also a disadvantage unless just small amounts are to be dried.

Convection Oven Dehydration

The temperature is too hot in some convection ovens to successfully dehydrate fruits—they taste cooked. The air moving in the oven helps dry vegetables evenly. Beef jerky dried in the convection oven was acceptable.

Also, there is the problem of how to use the oven for every-day preparation of food when it is in use as a dehydrator. It depends on individual circumstances, but the convection oven is not usually a good choice for service as a dehydrator.

Combination Microwave-Convection Oven Dehydration

This oven has more space but would be limited for drying lugs of food. Single people drying small amounts may be very happy with the unit.

Dehydrator with Moisture Probe

The question most often asked is, "How do I know when it is dry?" In the near future Alternative Pioneering Systems will be introducing a probe in their FD200 machine. Prototypes are being tested at the present time (1981). The probe is inserted into a vegetable or a piece of fruit in the dehydrator. The machine is set to indicate the moisture content desired and when the food reaches that degree of dryness it will automatically shut off. If the food is left unattended on a humid day and starts to reabsorb moisture, the dehydrator will turn back on and dry it out again. I am very anxious to get a unit to try.

A Look at Available Units

*Excalibur ED-301, ED-321**

Cabinet: steel; wood-grain vinyl covering
Dimensions: 12 × 22 × 17 inches deep
Capacity: nine plastic trays with 16 square feet of drying area (including the bottom)
Weight: 27 pounds
Warranty: 1 year
Suggested Price: ED-301, $139; ED-321 w/timer, $159

The Excalibur has an E-Z Off Door* for simple tray loading and cleaning. It has a fully adjustable thermostat for desired temperature setting with a drying guide for handy reference and model ED-321 has a 24-hour timer that can also be set to run continuously. The sturdy trays have polypropylene inserts that are dishwasher safe, and snap in and out with the touch of a finger for easy loading and cleaning. The units have triple protection against electrical failure, simple and reliable controls, scientifically designed triple air chambers and filtered air flow. The dehydrator sits conveniently on a countertop and looks like a microwave oven. It has horizontal air flow and the food drys faster when the trays are rotated 180° halfway through the drying process. Check the noise level for inside drying.

Excalibur ED-400A

Cabinet: wooden cabinet totally covered by vinyl laminate
Dimensions: 15 × 16½ × 19¼ inches deep
Capacity: ten E-Z clean drying trays with removable polypropylene inserts for 17 square feet of drying area
Weight: 30 pounds
Warranty: 1 year
Suggested Price: $159

This dehydrator is designed to handle volume output. It has a 10-inch fan and, according to the manufacturer, is the fastest dehydrator on the market. It has the same trays and inside cabinet as the ED-301, -321. It has an E-Z Off* lift-away door for fast and easy loading. It has triple protection against electrical hazards—hi-limit protection. It has a side on-off switch. The unit should be turned off before opening the door because of the amount of air flow. Check the noise level. This unit does not have a filter.

Excalibur ED-600

Cabinet: plastic and steel
Dimensions: 8 × 20 × 22 inches deep
Capacity: five plastic trays with approximately 8 square feet of drying area
Weight: 15 pounds
Warranty: 1 year
Suggested Price: $99

This is Excalibur's new compact unit. It has the same features as the 301. The fold-down/removable door is difficult to close. Drying time is cut down when the trays are rotated 180° halfway through the drying cycle. The advantage of this unit over other compact units on the market is the removable trays allowing bread raising, yogurt making and craft-project drying. Check the heat and the noise level of the unit. There is no filter on this machine.

*E-Z Off—trade name used by Excalibur Products.

Harvest Maid FD-300

Cabinet: steel with vinyl finish
Dimensions: 10½ × 21½ × 17½ inches deep
Capacity: eight plastic trays with 14 square feet of drying area (including the bottom)
Weight: 25 pounds
Warranty: 1 year
Suggested Price: $199

This unit offers adjustable filtered air flow, both horizontal and recirculating. It has a 600-watt heating element with solid state circuitry. The trays load and unload easily and have flexible removable mesh inserts. The trays have a tendency to sag. The on-off switch is independent of the adjustable thermostat. They are located on the front of the unit along with a drying guide with temperature settings. The door is not removable but opens to the left. A thermal cut-off shuts off the heater if a malfunction occurs. A half-cycle function automatically cuts in after the unit gets up to operating temperature. This unit will not accommodate peach halves, unless some of the trays are removed, because the shelves are closer together than in other units on the market. The heat and air flow are even and, in tests made by the author, drying was faster than other similarly designed units. Looks like a microwave oven.

Harvest Maid FD-200

Cabinet: steel with baked enamel finish
Dimensions: 10½ × 21½ × 17½ inches deep
Capacity: eight drying trays with 14 square feet of drying area (including the bottom)
Weight: 25 pounds
Warranty: 1 year
Suggested Price: $164.95

This unit has a double-wall construction to conserve energy. It has a pressurized air chamber. The air is drawn through a rear filter, heated and blown horizontally across the trays from right to left. It has the option of recirculating a portion of the air for energy savings. It has a white plastic interior for easy cleaning, the same as the FD-300 unit. It has high-limit protection. It did not dry as fast or as even as the FD-300 model and consumed more energy during the author's tests.

Harvest Maid Preserver FD-101

Cabinet: the base is steel and the top is high-impact plastic
Dimensions: 9½ inches high, 15 inches in diameter
Capacity: four one-square foot plastic trays with clean-a-screens; expandable to 12 trays total
Weight: 12 pounds
Warranty: 1 year
Suggested Price: $89

This compact unit has an adjustable thermostat and can be expanded from the 4 trays in the basic unit to 12 trays. It has horizontal air flow. The fan forces air up the outer chamber of each tray, then draws it horizontally across the tray into the core. Heat and air are distributed evenly across every tray. No tray rotation is needed to keep the bottom tray from scorching. Because the air flow is across the top of the tray it is possible to dry leathers without stopping the air flow as would happen in units where air flows through the trays. Constant air flow and pressure is assured by the interlocking self-sealing trays. A third exterior wall forms an insulating air pocket on the outside of the two interior walls. This reduces heat loss making the unit more energy efficient and also promotes faster drying. This machine is the second fastest dehydrator tested by the author. This was the quietest dehydrator the author tested. It has a high-limit protection.

Harvest Savor (manufactured by Telrob Corporation)

Cabinet: plastic
Dimensions: 12½ inches tall and 12 inches in diameter
Capacity: with the five trays, it is just under 4 square feet
Weight: 5 pounds with 5 trays
Warranty: 1 year
Suggested Price: $84.95

This unit comes with 5 stackable trays. The air flow is unique. The design diffuses the air across the trays. The unit operates from a 200-watt element and a small 4-inch fan. It has an impedance-protected motor. This unit dries fruits and vegetables with shelf rotation from top to bottom but it is hard to dry fruit leathers because the plastic wrap blocks the air flow when it is placed on the bottom tray of the dehydrator. This appears to be a popular dehydrator for high-humidity areas.

Little Harvey (manufactured by Harvest Company)

Cabinet: double steel-wall which allows good insulation with a painted outside surface
Dimensions: 17 × 13 × 24 inches deep
Capacity: eight screen trays that do not warp, providing 16 square feet of actual drying space (does not include bottom)
Weight: 36 pounds
Warranty: 30 months
Suggested Price: $169

All working components are on the back panel, should repair be necessary. This unit has a calrod heating element with a six-inch fan and horizontal air flow from rear to front. The controls on the unit are not on the front because the company feels the rear controls provide safety in operation, i.e., children cannot easily operate the unit. High limit protection is included with this unit. It has a combined on-off and temperature control. The metal tray gets hot and the screening has to be handled carefully but it dries evenly.

3

What's New In Pretreatment

The purpose of pretreatment is to help preserve color, nutrients, flavor and overall quality of the finished product. Specific vegetables and fruits are high in different vitamins. It is important to know how the vitamin is destroyed and what pretreatment will stop the loss. Home and Garden Bulletin Number 72, *Nutritive Value of Foods* (USDA, April 1977), gives a partial listing of the most common fruits and vegetables and what each food contains. It is important to know this information before pretreating foods to go into the dehydrator. Strawberries have a high vitamin C content. Vitamin C is destroyed by light, heat and oxygen; therefore, pretreatment by dipping in sodium bisulfite will help save the vitamin C in the strawberry.

Green beans have a high vitamin A content so they require steam blanching. They also have thiamin that would be destroyed if they were pretreated by dipping in sodium bisulfite. Vitamin A is not heat sensitive and steaming will stop the enzyme action that causes an off flavor. Green beans have minerals that can be dissolved if they are soaked in water or boiled; therefore, pretreatment by steam blanching or microwave blanching is the best method.

Steam blanching or microwave pretreatment is necessary for foods that have a tough, natural wax protective skin such as grapes. Pretreatment breaks down the waxy layer and crazes the skin, permitting a faster rate of moisture transfer to the surface of the fruit, and reduces the drying time.

Vitamin A is a fat-soluble vitamin and is not destroyed by blanching or soaking. Light can reduce the amount of vitamin A.

Vitamin C is sensitive to oxidation and heat. It is water soluble and is easily destroyed.

Thiamin is destroyed by sulfur compounds and is also water soluble and may be lost in soaking water.

The manuals that come with dehydrators should give tables specifying which method of pretreatment is best for the specific food.

It appears that there is no single method that is best for pretreatment of all foods. When dipping in sodium bisulfite, the color of the food and the vitamin C is protected but the thiamin is lost. Steaming protects the vitamin A but the vitamin C is reduced and the appearance isn't as appealing.

Select the pretreatment method that protects color, vitamins, or minerals as desired. If you do not know the predominate type of vitamins or minerals in the foods, refer to the appropriate references and pretreat accordingly.

It is possible to dry foods without pretreatment and retain a good color. However, the color will deteriorate during storage, thus shortening the shelf life. The browning reaction continues unless it is stopped by some type of pretreatment.

Vegetable Pretreatment

Blanching reduces microorganism growth that causes food spoilage, stops destructive chemical changes, helps retain vitamin A, preserves color, and makes the skin porous, allowing the food to dry faster. It also helps save the thiamin and carotene and removes air, preventing air pockets in the finished product.

Steam Blanching: Place 1 inch of water in a pan with a tight-fitting lid. Place 2 cups of sliced food into a steamer rack. When the water comes to a boil, place the rack into the pan and replace the lid. Steam until the vegetable is translucent or just tender. It requires a longer time for steam blanching at higher altitudes than it does near sea level.

Beans turn a vivid green, peas indent, the milk in the kernel of corn sets (turns to water). Beets and winter squash will have to be cooked until they are completely done.

Vegetables that require only a short cooking time (such as zucchini, peppers, onions, mushrooms, etc.), need only to be chopped, sliced, or diced and placed on the tray to dry.

Steam blanching is preferred to water blanching because less water soluble vitamins and minerals are lost.

If a microwave oven is available, it provides an easy method of pretreating vegetables. Because of lack of standardization of power levels with various microwave ovens, it is impossible to provide a pretreatment timetable that can be used with all ovens.

Prepare the vegetables just the same as for steam or water blanching. Place the food just one-layer deep. Set the oven on high. Use the fresh vegetable guide, but reduce the time about one-third because the vegetable should not be completely cooked—only tender. Use a dish with a lid, or cover the dish with plastic wrap. Set the microwave timer for half of the required time. When it goes off, stir the vegetables, transferring the outside food to the center and the center to the outside to permit a more uniform pretreatment for a more quality product. Transfer the food to the dehydrator tray and dry.

Microwave pretreatment preserves more nutrition because water is not added to the vegetable and the water soluble nutrients are not lost.

Bisulfite Steaming: Place ¼ teaspoon of sodium bisulfite into 1 cup of boiling water. Put prepared sweet potatoes or yams into the steamer and place the steamer into the pan of boiling water with a tight fitting lid. Steam until they are tender. Remove from the steamer and place into the dehydrator to dry. This combined method helps save the vitamin A and also some of the thiamin.

Fruit Pretreatment

Ascorbic and Citric Acid: Dissolve 1 tablespoon of citric and ascorbic acid in 2 quarts of water. Soak fruit in the solution for 2 minutes and drain thoroughly before placing on dehydrator trays. The combination of ascorbic and citric acid helps prevent browning.

Checking: Prunes, figs, plums, cranberries, grapes, etc., have a natural wax protective coating. It is necessary when drying these fruits whole to pretreat them by dipping them in boiling water for 1 to 2 minutes depending on the size and the toughness of the skin. This procedure is called checking or crazing the skin to allow the moisture to escape. It speeds the drying time.

Microwave Checking: Fruits that require checking/crazing, such as grapes, whole figs, prunes, etc., may be treated in the microwave. Use a microwave-safe dish and place the fruits one layer deep. Figs and prunes take about two minutes per square foot tray and grapes only take one minute. Set the timer for

1 minute and stir the prunes, or set it for 30 seconds and stir the grapes. Reset the timer for the remaining 1 minute or 30 seconds. Because of the air circulation in the dehydrator, it is not necessary to cool the foods that are pretreated. Just place the fruit on the trays to dry.

Sodium Bisulfite: Sodium bisulfite is a sodium carbonate solution saturated with sulfur dioxide gas and crystalized. When the sodium bisulfite crystals are placed in water, the sulfur dioxide dissipates into the air and combines with the oxygen surrounding the fruit. This helps prevent oxidation and preserves more of the natural vitamin C and color in the fruit. Dipping potatoes into a sodium bisulfite solution helps retain the vitamin C. Sodium bisulfite causes loss of thiamin and should not be used with vegetables containing thiamin.

Sodium bisulfite may be purchased at a chemical supply company, at wine-making supply stores, and at some drug store perscription counters. Do not confuse it with sodium sulfate (known as Glauber's salt), which is a cathartic and will cause diarrhea.

Use 1 teaspoon of sodium bisulfite dissolved in 1 quart of water. Soak for 2 minutes in the solution, drain thoroughly and place on the trays to dry. This amount will pretreat 20 pounds of fruit. Do not try to keep the solution to use at a later time because it loses its effectiveness when it is exposed to the air. This is a liquid form of sulfur. It helps retain vitamin C and keeps the color bright, but it will not penetrate the skin of some fruits such as apricots.

Caution: Do not use sodium bisulfite to retain color on food to be eaten fresh; fruit that is to be frozen; or food canned by boiling water, steam, or pressure-cooker methods.

Potassium Metabisulfite: This can be used in the place of sodium bisulfite for anyone that is restricted in sodium intake. This is available in small quantities from wine-making supply stores. Check with your physician for permission to avoid dietary inbalance.

Sulfuring: Sulfuring produces soft, pliable, pretty-colored fruit. Do not sulfur in your dehydrator. Obtain instructions from the Extension Service for building a sulfuring box or refer to *The ABC's of Home Food Dehydration* for complete instructions on how to do this. There are some specific instructions that must be followed for successful sulfuring procedures.

This is an especially good method to use in treating overripe fruits. It stops the enzyme action that causes browning and fruits have a higher sugar content when they are more ripe. If you desire to do halves of large fruits, it would be advisable to sulfur the fruits. It does not require as much sulfur for fruits to be dried in the dehydrator as for fruits dried in the sun. The sulfuring time is also reduced.

Granulated, dust-free, easily ignited burning sulfur is available for sulfuring fruit. It can be obtained from a ranch supply store.

4

What's New With Individual Foods

Apple Snax

When crispy dried Apple Snacks and Fruit Snacks came to market the telephone kept ringing, "Have you tasted that new apple? It is so crisp but so expensive. How is it done? Can I do it?" Well fortunately a young lady that purchased a dehydrator from me also wanted to know the answer to the question. She had worked in a dehydrated food plant and said she thought she could figure it out with some experimentation. She developed the technique. She dried the apples in the dehydrator and then placed them in the oven. She tried many temperature settings and after warping 2 trays because the oven was too hot, she finally got the right temperature—170° F. It takes approximately two hours for the moisture content to get down to two percent.

Place the apples on a cookie sheet, one layer deep, and bake until 98-99 percent of the moisture is removed. The first snacks had cinnamon sugar sprinkled on them and we discovered it was best to sprinkle the mixture over them before they were dried. With further experimentation we learned that flavored gelatin could make an apple taste like an apricot or a peach or a strawberry.

For people who do not want added sugar, it is possible to use D-Zerta* and get the same results with less calories.

Apricots

When I first started to teach food dehydration classes, people always asked if I could dry apricots like those that could be purchased in the market. Yes, my apricots were pretty

---

*D-Zerta is a product of General Foods Corporation, White Plains, N.Y.

because I dried them while they were firm, but they did not have the flavor of a juicy ripe apricot, and they turned brown in storage.

I was very adamant when I first started drying fruits with regard to pretreatment. In no way was I going to add anything to my food except ascorbic acid, fruit juice or honey.

Winters, California, is a big producer of dried apricots. Apricots are sulfured and placed in the sun to dry. From the middle of June to the middle of July, Winters has to be the "Sulfur Capitol" of the world. Everyone is sulfuring apricots and the air is filled with the fumes of sulfur. Native Californians often suggested to me that if I would try sulfuring I would be happy with the results, especially for apricots.

One day I visited a farm in my area that drys and markets dried apricots. I watched the workers cut the apricots and place them on huge screen trays in the sun to dry. I asked the farmer if I could buy some apricots to experiment with. He was reluctant because he said, "Apricots are California gold." I persisted and he finally allowed me to purchase a small lug.

When I got home and started to work with the cots I was sick! Some of them looked like they should be thrown away. Then I decided maybe I could make jam or leather with them. I pondered my dilemma and finally decided that if, commercially, they had success drying apricots that looked like that, then I should at least give it a try. My husband helped me make a sulfuring box and I got the trays loaded. Then I tried to start the sulfur. After holding my breath so long that I almost turned black in the face, I finally got the sulfur to burn. I then retreated to the house to escape the fumes and wait.

An hour later, when I removed the cardboard box and saw those apricots, I was ecstatic. Beautiful light-colored juicy apricots came into view. I quickly transferred them onto the dehydrator trays and placed them into the dehydrator to dry. I moved the dehydrator outside because I didn't want sulfur fumes in my home. Twenty hours later I had pretty orange, pliable, flavorful apricots—far prettier than anything I could buy. Sulfur bleaches, and helps prevent enzyme action and nonenzymatic browning. This pretreatment helps reduce the loss of vitamin A and vitamin C, and removes air from the tissues. The burning sulfur penetrates the skin and helps keep the color. I now sulfur all of my apricots, which are purchased very ripe. They keep their beautiful color until the next season. When people ask that question I can now say as I puff with pride, "Yes, my apricots are even prettier than those purchased in the market."

Banana Chips

"I love the banana chips you buy at the store. They are so crisp!" I heard that statement so many times that it became a challenge to me to find the secret. I tried deep frying, baking on a greased cookie sheet, etc. Finally I discovered that the banana used commercially was not the same one I was purchasing at the market, but a large banana called the Plantain, with flavoring and sugar added. I ordered a whole case (the smallest amount I could special order from San Francisco). Because of the starch content, they dry more crisp, but they taste like a potato. I bought the commercial chips and tasted them, trying to copy them. I added honey to sweeten and they tasted like honey instead of bananas. I deep fried them after I had soaked them in Karo Syrup, but they were greasy after they were dried. The kids in the neighborhood ran when I went outside because they were sick of tasting bananas.

I batted zero. I had one that was pretty close to the commercial banana that I soaked in Karo and banana oil flavoring but it was just not quite as thin and crisp. I decided that I didn't like banana oil flavoring and I didn't want added sugar, so I gave up.

After I learned about baking the apples, I started using that same process for bananas. By slicing the bananas 1/16-inch thick, dipping them in sodium bisulphite, drying them and then baking them at 170° F. for 2 hours or until they were crisp, I had a good product.

To keep them crisp, it is best to seal them in a heat-sealable bag, or vacuum seal them for long time storage. If they soften because of high humidity, just place them in the oven again and heat until they are crisp.

Cherries

To maintain a good-flavored dried cherry it is important to watch the temperature carefully. It takes cherries a long time to dry because they have a natural wax protection. If they are to be dried whole, it is necessary to pretreat them by dipping them in boiling water for two minutes or placing them in the microwave for one minute. This is one fruit that cannot be rushed.

It is not necessary to pretreat cherries if they are pitted before they are dried. Do not use the recycle mode when drying cherries. Set the dehydrator at 130° F. and be patient. It will take about 24 hours for a full dehydrator load to dry. Toward the end of the drying time, check the cherries by letting them cool to room temperature. They will be like a miniature dried prune.

Leathers

When I first started making leather rolls, they all looked alike. The apricot, peach, pumpkin, persimmon and nectarine were all brown. The apple, pear, and banana were all a little lighter shade of brown. The strawberry and plum were deep red. Everything had to be labeled in order to determine what flavor it was. A friend called and said, "Barbara, I used a whole bottle of Fruit Fresh in my apricot leather and it still turned brown. I am going to find a way to keep it light and I'll call you back." She called a few days later to report that she had brought the fruit to a boil and then dried it, and it held a pretty good color. So I started cooking all of my leathers with a high vitamin C content to stop the browning enzyme.

One day I wanted to make applesauce. My apple leather was discolored. I pondered that idea for awhile and thought about my apples and how pretty and white they were, so I made my applesauce from the apple slices. Finally the idea struck me. Why not dip the fruit for leather in sodium bisulfite to maintain the color? I tried it with apples and it was a perfect color. Then I tried it with some peaches and that also worked.

It is hard for me to comprehend why it took me so long to realize what was happening to my fruit leathers. So many times I placed pretty-colored fruit in my blender and then watched it discolor as I turned on the blender and whipped oxygen into the fruit, destroying the natural vitamin C.

By soaking the blemished fruits in sodium bisulfite for 2 minutes, draining them before placing them into the blender to puree them, and placing 2 cups of puree per standard-size dehydrator tray, the end result is a nutritious, pretty-colored roll of fruit with a higher natural vitamin C content. Such a simple solution to the problem!

Sweet Potatoes or Yams

When pretreating food, it is important to know the vitamin content and how the vitamin is destroyed that is present in the food. Sweet potatoes and yams have high vitamin A, vitamin C and thiamin. The pretreatment that will save the vitamin A is steaming, but steaming destroys vitamin C. To dip in sodium bisulfite retains vitamin C but destroys thiamin.

The solution for this problem is to pretreat by steaming over sodium bisulfite water. Not all vegetables require a double pretreatment, but if it will help save the nutritional value and preserve flavor and color, then it is well worth the effort to provide proper pretreatment. Sweet potatoes, when pretreated in this manner, are flavorful from one season to the next.

Tomatoes

Have you ever had a tomato turn black and wondered why? They look terrible and even have a scorched flavor. I questioned why.

An article appeared in the newspaper cautioning home canners to add lemon juice or vinegar to their tomatoes to increase the acid content before they canned them to prevent spoilage. The article suggested that because some people do not like high-acid tomatoes, the seed companies have developed low-acid tomatoes, making it necessary to add acid (lemon juice or vinegar) to have the proper ph for canning. The article also indicated that the chemical balance of the tomato changed when it was left on the vine for extended periods of time, reducing the acid content.

Some of my tomatoes turned black and others didn't, which left me puzzled. I decided to experiment. I picked an Ace tomato from the vine that was pretty and red but firm. There was another one just like it on the vine, but to prove my point I left it on the vine for four more days. Then to make sure it would turn black when I dried it, I kept it on the cupboard for five days. Finally I sliced it up and placed it in the dehydrator to dry. What a shock! It was just as pretty as the first one I had dried. It did not turn black.

For the answer to my question as to why the tomatoe turned black, I went to the seed company and learned that the acid content of different varieties isn't that significant. The Italian pear tomato and the yellow varieties have a slightly lower acid content but the acidity is masked by sweetness. I stopped looking to the acid content as the determining factor in color change and started checking for other factors. All tomatoes that dry pretty and do not turn dark have the same characteristic—low moisture content. The Beefsteak tomato turned black almost every time I dried it, but the yellow, pear and Ace all kept their color.

I also tried some varieties that are grown for the cannery with a very low moisture content. They dried beautifully and held their color the whole year. All varieties that I have tested that dried with a good color were meaty, low moisture, mature and firm.

Check with the local county extension service to find the tomato that grows best, has a lot of meat and a low moisture content, and try it. I still have an occasional tomato turn black in spots because it was overripe when I placed it into the dehydrator.

Yogurt

A dehydrator dealer from the Bay area called me one afternoon. She had been camping at Tahoe and had car trouble, so while she was waiting to get the car fixed, we chatted. We were sharing our enthusiasm for drying and she told me about yogurt drops.

One of the men in the group made a remark about his distaste for yogurt at the beginning of their outing and she kept very quiet. He spent all weekend praising her for the candy she brought with her—it was lemon yogurt drops.

Many people that dislike yogurt eat dried yogurt. The drops are best when they are crisp. Yogurt leather rolls are also good. Measure 2 cups of flavored yogurt and spread onto a teflex sheet to dry. Remove it and roll in plastic wrap for storage.

Should you discover that you need a cup of flavored yogurt and you don't have any fresh, it can be reconstituted by breaking the roll in half, breaking one half into small pieces, placing it in the blender, adding water to the one-cup measure, and blending it into a smooth puree. The other half of the roll can be set aside for use at a later time.

Zucchini

The prolific, versatile zucchini is so mild it can be used as mock pineapple, pumpkin or tomato and never be recognized. It is almost impossible to make people believe they are, in fact, eating zucchini.

A friend from Utah sent me the recipe for mock pineapple to see what I could do with it. Dried Imitation Pineapple Drops were the hit of the year. When I serve pineapple drops at demonstrations I have many non-believers. They insist zucchini doesn't taste like that—it has to be pineapple.

The bigger the zucchini the better. Peel the zucchini and remove the seeds before grating it. I dried some and froze some to be dried later, to allow me to have pineapple drops year round.

Because of the low acid content of zucchini, it is important to process it at a temperature of 240° F. in a pressure canner at 10 pounds pressure at sea level (higher pressure at higher altitudes—check canner directions) for the required time. This method of preservation may be used by people that do not have freezer space available.

I grate my zucchini before I dry it and store it in a gallon jar. When I am ready to use it I just place the grated zucchini into the blender, add boiling water, let it stand a couple of minutes and puree it. By adding spices it becomes a good substitute for use in many recipes, such as mock pumpkin cake or pie, as an extender for tomato sauce or paste, and as a substitute for pineapple. It is not necessary to peel the zucchini if it is to be used to make cakes or cookies, but green pineapple or pumpkin would not look very appetizing.

5

What's New In Food Preparation

There are two steps in dehydration:

1. Removing water from the surface of the food.
2. Pulling the water from the center of the food to the surface, where it can then be removed by evaporation.

Three things affect the drying of food:

1. Humidity of the air.
2. Air flow and temperature within the dehydrator.
3. Moisture content and composition of the food to be dried.

Should moisture condense on the door of the dehydrator at the beginning of the drying cycle, it may be necessary to leave the door open to help move the moist air away from the food. After a few hours, sufficient moisture will have evaporated that the door may then be closed.

If the combination of air flow and temperature create drying conditions that are too rapid, the surface of the food may become too dry, thereby reducing the flow of moisture from the center of the food. This is known as case hardening.

By slicing food with a high moisture content into smaller pieces, it will dry faster. Pretreating foods with a natural wax protection can reduce the drying time.

Cutting Fruits and Vegetables for Dehydration

Most foods are difficult to cut into smaller pieces once they have been dehydrated. For ease of use at a later time, it is advisable to cut fresh fruits and vegetables into appropriate sizes at preparation time. Smaller sizes dehydrate and reconstitute more rapidly than larger ones. A general rule to follow is to cut produce into one-fourth to three-eights-inch pieces. Exceptions, of course, always exist. Cherries, plums, and apricots can be cut in half for easy removal of pits and they will dry faster than if they are left whole. To avoid having to pretreat figs, cut them in half to speed drying time. Prunes can also be cut in half to avoid pretreatment.

To dry stone fruits in circles, cut a slice from the stem end and lift out the pit and continue slicing in circles. Freestone plums, peaches, and nectarines look pretty sliced in circles.

Cut pears in half and remove the core by slicing from the stem end to the blossom end. Then make two more slices on each side of the half, parallel to the first cut, and the pear will dry faster. Pears can be sliced in circles if the core is not objectionable.

Apples may be peeled, cored and sliced with one easy operation when using an apple parer. They may also be cut in the same way pears are cut. Cut the apple in half from the stem end to the blossom end and make two more cuts parallel to the first cut on each side. This cuts down the slicing time and speeds the drying time.

There is a tomato slicing tool that is available from hardware and discount stores that is great for slicing tomatoes. Remove the stem and place the tomato on a cutting board. The slicer has a serrated edge and it slices the tomato into equal slices that dry quickly. It isn't necessary to remove the skin, but the two outside slices will take longer to dry so it is best to save them for making leather.

There are all kinds of slicing devices on the market for helping prepare food for the dehydrator. The most-used piece of equipment is a stainless steel paring knife. The opening in the food processor is not large enough to do whole fruits and to squeeze them into the opening sometimes mashes the fruit. Some people use egg slicers to slice soft fruits.

A *kernel cutter* that cuts all kernels from the ear of corn with one quick stroke is a must. There is one available that will expand to fit all size ears and by using it the corn does not get mashed or crushed but comes out in large kernels.

A *stainless steel steam basket* can be used to pretreat foods when a microwave is not available and it can also be used in reconstitution.

A *cherry stoner* cuts down the time of preparation and speeds the drying time for cherries.

A *colander* for draining fruits is convenient. It should be either stainless steel or plastic.

Three bowls for preparing fruit are convenient when pretreating. Prepare and slice into one bowl while the fruit in the other bowl is soaking. Place the soaked fruit into the colander, letting it drain over the third bowl. There is one bowl soaking, one bowl draining and one bowl to slice into. By rotating in this manner, the fruit can be placed on the tray as it is ready and, should an emergency arise, the whole operation can stop without losing the nutritional value of the food.

A *blender* is very helpful in preparing fruit leathers. It is very essential in reconstituting fruits and vegetables for making soups, sauces, butters, and fruit-flavored shakes.

A good pair of *kitchen shears* is necessary when cutting dehydrated foods for cakes, cookies, granola, etc.

Cuts for Fast Dehydration

By slicing the pear in this manner, it keeps the slices uniform and they dry evenly.

Remove the cap of the strawberry and slice in 3 or 4 equal pieces, depending on the size.

Use an apple parer. It peels, cores and slices apples in one easy operation.

For less slicing, cut in half and remove core; make 2 more slices on each side.

Peaches may be cut in half and sliced like the pear and apple, or they can have the top slice removed, allowing the pit to be lifted out, and then sliced in circles.

Use a tomato slicing knife, available from hardware stores, to slice the tomato with one cut.

Equipment for Use in Preparing Foods for Dehydration and Storage

Kernel Cutter

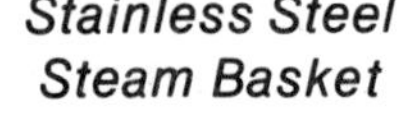

Stainless Steel Steam Basket

Cherry Stoner

Vacuum Sealer

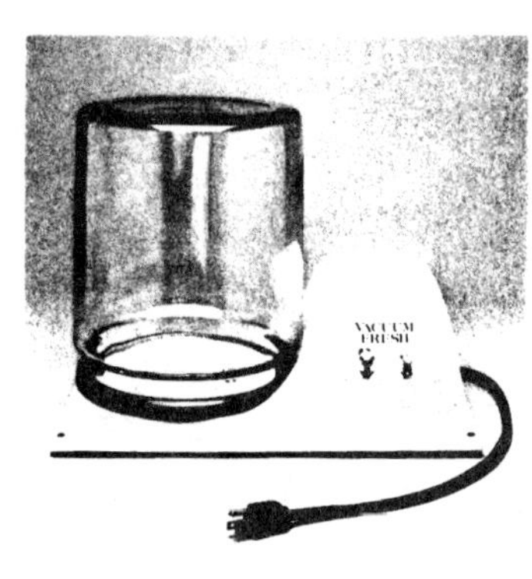

Apple Parer

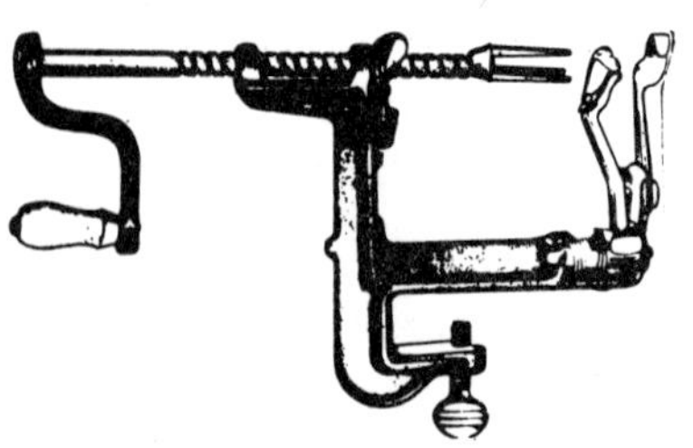

Heat Sealer for Plastic Pouches

6

Guidelines For Food Purchasing

It is difficult to suggest amounts of food to purchase for dehydration because of the variables involved. A LA lug (small) holds approximately 20-24 pounds of fruit. A field lug (large) contains from 40-44 pounds of fruit. A bushel holds approximately 40-44 pounds of fruit. These measures vary because they are volume measures. If the fruit is large, it will fill the container without as much weight as if it were small and more compact.

Some of the variables to be considered are: how ripe the food is, pretreatment, the sugar content, the size of slices, and the amount of discard in preparation. Other factors are the outside temperature, the humidity of the air, the moisture content of the food, and how fast the food dries. These things all have to be considered before the quantity can be determined.

An example would be tomatoes. They have very little waste, with a very high moisture content, while apples have quite a bit of waste (peels, core, and stem) with a lower moisture content. Another thing to remember—some products can be held for a few weeks before processing, while others can only be held a few days. Apples can be dehydrated over a period of weeks without noticeable loss of quality, but tomatoes have to be processed within a few days.

A screen tray that has one square foot of surface will hold about 1½ pounds of food. A tray made out of more rigid material, such as molded plastic or aluminum, will hold approximately 2 pounds of food. This, of course, is speaking of fruit halves, not thin slices or small cherries or berries. Large pear slices would also consume more space for their weight because of the size. If the dehydrator capacity is 20 pounds, do not purchase three field lugs of apricots at the same time to dehydrate because that dehydrator is not capable of drying that much fruit while it is in prime condition. The preparation discard on apricots is only about 10 percent. With bananas it is 45-50 percent, because of the weight of the skins.

Consider the suggestions above and use wise judgment when purchasing quantities of food for dehydration.

7

High Altitude Corrections

The recipes in this book have been tested at sea level. For successful use of the recipes at higher altitudes, the following information will be helpful.

Boiling and Moist Heat Cooking: At or near sea level, water boils at 212° F. Because of atmospheric pressure at higher altitudes, liquids may be at a "bubbling boil" and still be cooler than 212° F. As the altitude increases, it requires a longer boiling time for the food to become tender.

Candies and Jams: The cold-water test is reliable. However, when using a thermometer, it is necessary to make corrections. Measure the boiling temperature of water for the elevation and subtract that temperature reading from 212° F. Subtract this temperature correction from the recipe temperature. As an example, at 5,000 feet elevation water boils at 203° F. Subtract 203° from 212° *F. The temperature correction* is 9 degrees. When a recipe requires cooking to 239° F., subtract the 9 degrees from 239 degrees and cook to 230° F. Use this same method for correcting other recipes developed at sea level.

Batters and Doughs: Baking powder, soda, yeast, or even air beaten into batter, exerts more push on the cell walls at higher elevations. If the batter has a coarse, crumbly texture or overflows the pan, the elevation could be the cause. Recipes using baking powder or soda as a levening agent need more adjustment than yeast or air.

Angel Food Cakes: Avoid overbeating egg whites because the air beaten into the batter will expand the volume. Reduce the sugar slightly. Bake the cake at a higher temperature for a shorter time.

Cakes: Reduce baking powder by 1/8 teaspoon at 3,000 feet and by ¼ teaspoon at 7,000 feet per each teaspoon called for in the recipe. For each cup of sugar, decrease by 1 tablespoon for 3,000 feet and by 3 tablespoons for 7,000 feet. Increase the liquid by 1-2 tablespoons at 3,000 feet, and 3-4 tablespoons at 7,000 feet, for each cup of liquid. The liquid in the cake evaporates faster at higher elevations, causing the sugar to become more concentrated. This weakens the cell walls of the cake. Flour also dries out faster in higher elevations, so more liquid is required.

Biscuits, Muffins and Quick Breads: Because the texture is not so delicate, they probably will not require a change. If a change is needed, reduce the amount of baking powder.

Cookies: The recipe may be improved by reducing the baking powder and sugar slightly.

Breads: Yeast doughs rise faster at higher elevations. Use a little less flour and let the dough rise until double in bulk.

Baking Temperatures: No change is required from sea level to about 3,000 feet, but increase the baking temperature about 25 degrees for altitudes above that. Glass pans require a 25-degree lower baking temperature than metal pans. To prevent sticking, use well-greased pans dusted with flour (with the exception of angel or sponge cakes which should not be greased).

Using the above information, experiment and make notations. It may take two or three trys to discover the best proportions, but sea-level recipes can be adjusted for use at higher altitudes.

8

What's New In Storage

Labeling

Dehydrated foods should be labeled with date, contents and type of cut (halves, cubes, slices, grated) so they can be rotated. This enables the food dated earliest to be used first. Good organization and proper labeling of food eliminates guesswork and frustration. Some herbs look alike, and some leathers look alike after they are dried. It is necessary to taste them to distinguish between them. A few minutes spent in labeling is worth the effort because strawberry-rhubarb looks like strawberry, pumpkin and persimmon are look-alikes, and so are plum and cherry.

Packaging

Any container that has been used previously for food storage, that is air tight, moisture proof, and insect and rodent proof, can be used for dehydrated food storage.

Shortening and coffee cans with tight-fitting plastic lids are good containers. Recycled plastic or glass salad dressing, pickle or mustard bottles, and number-ten metal cans from restaurants, are also good.

Large plastic buckets with air-tight sealing lids will accommodate many pounds of food. When storing in metal cans, it is wise to put a plastic bag in the can to keep the food from touching the metal. When storing in a glass container, a plastic bag liner may save the food from shattered glass contamination should the jar be accidentally dropped or broken.

Heat-sealable plastic bags offer good protection from air and moisture if the air is pressed out before the bag is sealed. Some plastic pouches consist of two layers of plastic, polyester and polyolefin, bonded together for strength and impermeability. The result is a completely air-tight seal. Foods stored in these bags will last longer than the same foods stored in other containers. They also resist tearing, puncturing and the effects of heat and cold. They can be used for freezing, boil-in-the-bag foods, and microwaving. Plastic bags must be stored in an additional container that is insect proof, unless they are stored in the freezer.

Storage

The biggest concern with maintaining the nutritional value of home dehydrated foods is storage. Proper storage is essential if the food is to retain its nutritional value, maintain its color, not lose its flavor, and be free of contamination. The better the storage condition, the longer the food will remain in choice condition. Avoid light, heat, moisture, air and contamination when storing dehydrated food.

Light

Dehydrated foods exposed to light lose color, flavor and nutrition. Food should be protected by storing in a dark place or by using opaque containers. Aluminum foil or black plastic wrapped around the outside of glass jars will help protect the food from light. Aluminum pouches are good also.

Heat

Ideally, dehydrated food should be stored at 50° F. to 60° F. Well ventilated fruit cellars or basements provide good storage conditions. Do not store food in the garage or in a utility room with a washer and dryer where the temperature and humidity is constantly changing. Foods stored above the refrigerator, freezer or stove are exposed to unnecessary heat.

Moisture

When vegetables are dried they should have no more than 5 percent moisture for shelf storage. The moisture content can be increased to 10 percent for vegetable storage in the freezer. Fruits may have 10 percent moisture for shelf storage but can have 20 to 25 percent if they are to be stored in the freezer. Do not store food containers on cement floors. Elevate them on a board so they will not take on moisture.

Air

Freezer Storage: More moisture can be left in fruit and vegetables that are going to be stored in the freezer. Plastic boiling pouches do not breathe like other plastic bags; therefore, if the pouch is squeezed tightly against the food in the bag, the air will be forced out. When the bag is heat-sealed, it will be almost air free, and will remain air free until it is opened. The food will be protected from air, heat, moisture, light and contamination by insects. Dehydrated food does not require as much storage space as fresh food, so more food can be stored in limited freezer space. It is not necessary to pasteurize or equalize foods being stored in the freezer.

Dry Ice Storage: It is possible to seal foods for storage by using dry ice.

Large Containers: For long time storage of a large quantity of food, choose large plastic buckets with an air-tight sealing lid. Cover the bottom of the container with food. Then add one cubic inch of dry ice per quart. Place the ice in between several layers of newspaper and break it into small pieces with a hammer. Sprinkle it over the layer of food. Finish filling the container with food and place the lid on loosely to allow excess gas to escape. When all of the solid carbon dioxide has turned to gas and gas is no longer being expelled from the container, seal the lid. As a precaution, check after 15 minutes to make sure the lid is not bulged. If the lid is bulged, unseal it for a few minutes to let excess gas escape before trying to seal again.

Small Containers: To use glass jars, follow the same instructions, making sure the dry ice does not come in contact with the glass. Screw the lid on until it starts to tighten, then unscrew it slightly to allow excess gas to escape.

Caution: *Do not* touch dry ice with bare hands because it freezes the skin. *Do not* let dry ice touch glass, it may break. *Do not* seal containers until all excess gas from the dry ice escapes.

Food stored in this manner will be protected from most air, contamination by insects, light if stored in an opaque container, and moisture unless the container is breathable. The food should be equalized and pasteurized before placing into storage.

Vacuum Sealed Storage: Until now, vacuum packing has been available only in industry. But a home vacuum sealer is now on the market which uses recycled cans, canning jars, or any empty jar that has a rubber seal in its lid. The containers can be used over and over again.

The vacuum sealer has a bar attachment that is used for vacuum sealing heat-sealable bags. The bar clamp is placed at the top of the plastic bag and it is placed in the vacuum jar where the air is vacuumed out. The bag is then quickly sealed with a heat sealer. The most effective method of storage is vacuum-sealed dehydrated food stored in the freezer. Because the air has been vacuumed out of the bag it can not draw moisture from the food to form a frost in the package (freezer burn). It is maintained at a constant temperature and it is protected from light and moisture.

Not everyone can afford a vacuum sealer, but it is an ideal way to store dehydrated foods. Vacuum sealing also increases the life of foods stored on the shelf because it eliminates air, possible contamination by insects, and intrusion of moisture. It does require protection from heat and also light when stored in glass containers. Aluminum pouches are available especially to protect dehydrated food from light in storage. It is not necessary to equalize or pasteurize vacuum-sealed foods.

Contamination

How does contamination happen? Contamination is a waste of good food and also the time and money spent in preparing it.

Mold: To prevent mold contamination, food packaged for storage on the shelf should be very dry. Mold is not usually a problem unless moisture condenses on the foods. Food stored in a metal can is susceptible to mold caused by condensation because of temperature fluctuations. To prevent this, use a plastic bag liner inside the metal can.

Check the food when taking it out of the dehydrator for pieces that are too moist. Return the moist food to the dehydrator and continue to dry it. Place the other food loosely into a container with a tight lid and let it *equalize* for several days. The moisture from the underdried (10 percent moisture) pieces will be absorbed by the overdried (5 percent moisture) pieces. Each day, shake or stir the food to separate the pieces. When the pieces do not stick together they can be packaged for storage. If they are too sticky, return them to the dehydrator to remove excess moisture. Food that is to be vacuum-sealed (not heat-sealable pouches) or stored in the freezer does not need to be equalized.

Insects: When food is washed in preparation for dehydration, it isn't always possible to remove insect eggs. Even though the fruits and vegetables are washed thoroughly, it is possible for undetected eggs to remain on the food. When the food is put into storage and the temperature and moisture reach the right condition, the egg hatches and contaminates the food.

In some dehydrators it is possible for the food to become contaminated when it is left in the dehydrator with the heat and fan turned off. Insects fly into the dehydrator, deposit their eggs and fly off. Unknowingly the food is placed in storage and when the eggs hatch the food becomes contaminated.

A solution to this problem is to pasteurize the food before storing it. There are two methods that can be used to *pasteurize* food.

Freezer Method: To destroy eggs, place the dehydrated food in the freezer for two days or until the center of the food has reached 0° F. It is then safe to store it on the shelf in an insect-proof container. The freezing compartment of a refrigerator does not reach a low enough temperature to destroy the eggs.

Oven Method: Place the dehydrated food in a single layer on a cookie sheet and put it in the oven at 175° F. for 15 minutes. Heat causes some loss of nutritional value but it is better than losing the food to insects. It is then safe with either method to store the food on the shelf in an insect-proof container. (If the lid is left off from the storage container, insects can also contaminate the food.)

Storage Tips

1. Plan to store food from season to season only. Some foods deteriorate more rapidly than others. Do not discard food left from the previous year unless it obviously looks or tastes bad. Plan to use it before using the new dehydrated food because flavor, color, and nutrition do not improve with age.

2. To avoid flavor and moisture transfer, do not store fruits and vegetables in the same container unless they are heat sealed in air-tight pouches.

3. Fill containers as full as possible without crushing the food. The more food there is in a container, the less air there is to cause deterioration.

4. Package food in different size containers. Use small containers for immediate use and larger containers for long-time storage. After a container seal is broken, the food is susceptible to deterioration unless it is resealed.

5. Do not store herbs in paper bags. The paper absorbs the oils from the leaves and they lose their flavor.

6. Do not store dehydrated meats, fish, poultry, casseroles, soups, breakfast rolls with egg, or fruit rolls with spices and nuts for extended periods of time unless they are stored in a freezer. These foods should only be dried for convenience such as backpacking, camping or for use within a month's time to prevent off-flavors that develop because of chemical changes.

9

What's New In Reconstitution

When food is dehydrated the water is evaporated and, consequently, the cell walls collapse. When food is reconstituted it cannot rebuild the cell walls; therefore, the texture is different. This difference is especially noticeable in products which are usually eaten raw. Cucumber, spinach and tomato cannot be reconstituted to the texture desired for a crisp salad, but they can be used in seasoning or in recipes where the food is cooked.

The moisture content of home dehydrated food varies considerably. It is not like commercially-dehydrated food where the moisture content is strictly controlled and maintained through proper packaging. The variance may be due to the length of dehydration time, humidity, or quality of storage conditions.

The art of reconstituting home dehydrated fruit or vegetables for use in favorite recipes is complicated by these factors. When substituting types of fruits or vegetables for those specified in the recipe, adjustments in moisture required for reconstitution may be necessary. An example would be the substituting of dates for apricots that are low in moisture content.

It is important to know the volume of fresh fruit used in creating a given quantity of dehydrated product. This will permit substitution of the proper amount of dehydrated food for the quantity of fresh food called for in the recipe. For example, a dehydrated persimmon is cut into 5 or 6 circles. One fresh persimmon makes 1 cup of puree which is the amount required to make steamed pudding. To substitute 10 pieces of persimmon would overpower the pudding with persimmon flavor. To use dehydrated food place the 5 pieces of persimmon into a blender, add water to the 1 cup measure and puree. This can then replace 1 cup of fresh pureed persimmon to make a delicious steamed pudding.

To soften fruit for use in cookies, candy, or cakes, place it in a steamer over one inch of water and allow it to steam for three minutes. Use kitchen shears to cut the fruit into bite-size pieces. For hors d' oeuvres made from fruit halves, steam the fruit but do not fill it with cheese until just before serving or the fruit will draw moisture from the cheese and it will crack and look stale.

To soften fruit for snacks, put a cup of fruit into a zip-lock bag with 2 or 3 drops of water or a piece of damp paper towel and place it in the refrigerator overnight. Unless the reconstituted fruit will be used within 2 or 3 days, it should be kept under refrigeration.

To make shakes, sauces, ice cream topping, baby food, puddings, cream soups, etc., use fruit or vegetable leathers. A two-cup roll of leather should be broken into pieces and placed in the blender. Add water to the two-cup measure and puree. This will be equivalent to the original two cups of fruit. To have a more concentrated sauce reduce the amount of water. When making baby food, it may be necessary to add more milk or water to make it more bland. Slices of fruit or vegetable can also be used as above by placing one cup into the blender, adding water to the one-cup measure and blending to make one cup of apple sauce, pear sauce, etc.

To reconstitute dried vegetables, meats or fruits to be used in cooking, place the food in a bowl, cover it with boiling water and soak it for five to twenty minutes. It is then ready to be used in the recipe. When reconstituted food is to be served cold, use cold liquid for reconstituting.

When reconstituting mushrooms for pizza, soak the mushrooms for five minutes, then drain, and use the water to reconstitute the tomatoes for the sauce. Never throw away the water-soluble vitamins and minerals from the soaking water. Save them for a stock pot. Do not use large amounts of water to reconstitute foods. It is always possible to add water, but it is a waste of nutrition to use too much water and discard it.

Sometimes it is necessary to use more dehydrated fruit slices than would be required fresh to have the necessary volume. Apple or peach pies, to look appetizing, must be full to the top. Because the fruit does not reconstitute to the original size, it is necessary to use more fruit. When serving the pie, cut the pieces smaller because the concentrated fruit is very rich and filling.

By following the guidelines above, it is possible to substitute dehydrated foods for fresh foods in favorite family recipes.

Enjoy the recipes in this book, and try new ones. Good luck!

PART 2

Apricot Pie

Broccoli Soup

Pizza, Tomatoes, Mushrooms

Bottle of Dehydrated Apples
(4 years old)

Pear Bread and Chocolate Zucchini Cake

Strawberry Milkshake

RECIPES

Alfalfa Sprout Dip (1)

1 pt sour cream
2 Tbsp powdered bouillon
2 Tbsp instant minced onion
1 tsp Mei Yen seasoning*

Mix well and add ½ to 1 cup of chopped alfalfa sprouts. A bouillon cube may be mashed and substituted for each tablespoon of powdered bouillon.

Cottage cheese pureed in blender may be substituted for sour cream.

Use dehydrated carrot, zucchini or tomato chips to dip into sauce.

*Mei Yen seasoning is a Spice Island spice.

Almonds (General Instructions) (2)

The hulls of almonds are green, fuzzy and oval shaped. Nuts should be harvested when the nuts in the center of the tree are ripe. When the nuts remain on the tree, the hulls split open and the shells and kernels begin to dry. The nuts are harvested by knocking them off from the tree. Nuts which fall to the ground should be cleaned up daily to prevent disease. The hulls should be removed and the nuts should be placed in the dehydrator at 100° F. and dried.

Because almonds are hard, they are one nut that can be chopped in the blender. To chop almonds, process no more than ½ cup at a time for half a minute on the highest speed. Other nuts should be shredded or grated with a sharp grinder. When nuts are crushed their oils are released and they become too oily.

Sprouted almonds are exceptionally crisp. They are good used in salads and to eat as a snack food. Soak 1 cup of raw almonds in tepid water overnight. Place in sprouter and drain. Rinse 3 times a day with tepid water and make sure they are well drained. As soon as the sprout breaks through the end of the kernel, they are ready to eat.

Blanching Almonds (3)

Cover almonds with water and heat to boiling. Drain immediately, then slip skins from almonds by pressing between thumb and fingers. Place almonds on absorbent paper or cloth to dry.

Caramelized Almonds (4)

Caramelize 1 cup slivered, blanched almonds by placing ¼ cup sugar and almonds in frying pan over low heat. Stir constantly until sugar melts and caramelizes. Remove from heat and spread on waxed paper to cool. Break apart. Use as a garnish for desserts.

Coconut Covered Almonds (5)

Dip slivered almonds into mixture for 10 minutes.

- ⅓ cup honey
- 1 cup water

Roll almonds in:

- 1 cup powdered sugar (sifted)
- 1 cup dehydrated grated coconut

Place in dehydrator at 130° F. and dry until crisp on outside (approximately 5 hours).

Toasted Almonds (6)

Place shelled almonds on a cookie sheet in oven at 300° F. for 25 to 30 minutes. Stir occasionally. Remove from oven and spread on paper towel to cool. To make toasted, blanched almonds, blanch the almonds and then toast them.

Apple-Apricot Bread (7)

- ⅔ cup milk
- 2 cups sifted flour
- 2½ tsp baking powder
- ½ tsp salt
- ½ tsp cinnamon
- ¾ cup sugar
- 1 cup dried, steamed, diced apples
- 1 cup dried, steamed apricots, finely diced
- ¼ tsp soda
- ½ tsp allspice
- ½ cup shortening
- 1 egg beaten
- ⅓ cup walnuts, chopped

Cream shortening; add sugar gradually while continuing to cream. Beat in egg. Add sifted dry ingredients alternately with liquid. Combine apples, apricots and walnuts; fold in. Spoon into a well-greased 8 x 5 x 3-inch loaf pan. Bake at 350° F. for 55 to 60 minutes or until loaf tests done. Turn out of pan; let cool.

Apple Butter (8)

- 4 cups dehydrated gravenstein apples, well packed
- 1/8 tsp salt
- 1/4 tsp cinnamon
- 1/8 tsp allspice
- 1/8 tsp cloves
- 2 cups apple cider, or 1/2 cider and 1/2 water
- 1 cup sugar (optional as desired)

Soak apples in hot cider for 10 minutes. Place in blender and puree until smooth. Add spices and sugar. Blend until thoroughly mixed. Place in jar and store in refrigerator.

Apple Crisp (Microwave) (9)

- 3 cups dehydrated apple slices
- 1/4 cup granulated sugar
- 1/2 tsp cinnamon
- 1/4 tsp cloves
- 2 tsp lemon juice
- 1/2 cup packed brown sugar
- 3/4 cup sifted flour
- 1/2 tsp salt
- 1/2 cup margarine/butter
- 1/4 cup chopped nuts

Place dehydrated apple slices in a 4-cup measure. Add boiling water to the 3-cup measure mark. Let stand 10 minutes to reconstitute. Combine sugar, cinnamon, cloves, and lemon juice and mix with fruit including any remaining water; place in 8 x 8-inch glass baking dish. Crumble together with fork the brown sugar, flour, salt, and butter. Mix in nuts and sprinkle over apples. Cook uncovered 8 to 10 minutes or until apples are tender. Serves 6.

Apple Custard Pie (10)

- 3 1/2 cups dehydrated sliced apples (reconstituted)
- 1 9-inch unbaked pie shell
- 1/4 tsp salt
- 3/4 tsp cinnamon
- 1/3 cup honey
- 2 eggs
- 1/3 cup honey
- 1 tsp vanilla
- 1/4 tsp salt
- 3/4 cup creamed cottage cheese
- 1 cup spiced apple yogurt (see recipe #17)

Place apples into pie shell. Combine salt, cinnamon and 1/3 cup honey; pour over apples. Bake at 425°F. for 15 minutes.

Beat eggs and 1/3 cup honey together slightly. Add vanilla, salt and cottage cheese. Beat with mixer until quite smooth. Add yogurt. Pour over apples in crust. Reduce oven temperature to 325°F. and continue baking 40 minutes or until set. Cool before serving.

Apple Date Butter (11)

- 2 cups pitted dates, snipped in half
- 2½ cups tart dehydrated Gravenstein apple slices
- 2 cups water
- Grated rind of 1 lemon
- ¼ tsp allspice
- ¼ tsp nutmeg
- ½ tsp cloves

Place all ingredients in a large saucepan. Mix well. Cook, uncovered, over medium heat, stirring frequently, until apples are tender and mixture is thick and uniform, about 25 minutes. Puree in blender. Spoon into hot sterilized jars; seal immediately, or cover with plastic wrap and refrigerate. Makes 3 cups.

Crunchy Dried Apple Dessert (12)

Reconstitute 6 cups of apple slices in 2½ cups of boiling water for 10 minutes. Stir occasionally so all apples will have an opportunity to rehydrate. Spread into a 9 x 13-inch oblong baking pan. Cover with the remaining juice (approximately ½ cup) and sprinkle with ¼ cup of granulated sugar and 1 teaspoon of cinnamon.

In a separate bowl, mix with a fork until crumbly:

- 1 egg slightly beaten
- 1 cup sugar
- 1 cup flour
- 1 tsp nutmeg
- 1 tsp baking powder
- ½ tsp salt

When it is very crumbly, sprinkle it over the top of the apples. Bake at 400° F. for 30 minutes, or until the apples are tender and the crust is browned.

For variety, add ½ cup crunchy (nut variety) granola to the above mixture before baking.

Crazy Crust Apple Pie (13)

Crust

- 1 cup flour
- 1 tsp baking powder
- ½ tsp salt
- 1 Tbsp sugar
- 1 egg
- ⅔ cup shortening
- ¾ cup water

Filling

- 3½ cups dehydrated apple slices
- 2¼ cups water
- ⅓ cup sugar
- 1¼ Tbsp cornstarch
- 2 Tbsp cold water
- ½ tsp apple pie spice
- 1 Tbsp lemon juice
- ½ tsp lemon rind

In small mixing bowl, combine flour, baking powder, salt, sugar, egg, shortening and water. Blend well; beat 2 minutes at medium speed of mixer. Pour batter into a 9-inch deep dish pie pan.

To make pie filling from dehydrated apples, combine 3½ cups dehydrated apple slices, 2¼ cups water and ⅓ cup sugar. Place in pan on surface unit and simmer until tender. Thicken with 1¼ tablespoons of cornstarch dissolved in 2 tablespoons cold water. Add lemon juice, spice, and rind. Mix well and pour filling into center of batter. Do not stir. Bake at 400° F. for 45 to 50 minutes.

Dutch Apple Pudding (14)

- 2 slices toasted bread, cut in 1-inch cubes
- 1 cup evaporated milk
- ½ cup water
- ¾ cup sugar
- 1½ cups dried apple slices, steamed and cut-up
- ½ cup brown sugar, packed
- ½ tsp nutmeg
- ¼ tsp salt
- 5 eggs
- 1 tsp cinnamon
- ½ cup raisins
- ½ cup chopped nuts

Put bread cubes, evaporated milk and water into a 3-quart bowl. Let stand 10 minutes. Beat eggs in a 1½-quart bowl until foamy. Stir remaining ingredients, except brown sugar, into eggs. Stir egg mixture into bread mixture. Pour into a buttered 2-quart baking dish. Sprinkle brown sugar over top. Bake at 300° F. for 45 to 50 minutes. Serve with Lemon Sauce (see recipe #158).

Apple-Raisin Sauce (Microwave) (15)

- ¼ cup brown sugar
- 1 Tbsp cornstarch
- ⅛ tsp salt
- ⅛ tsp allspice

Combine above ingredients in a 1-quart glass casserole. Add 1 cup apple juice and microwave on high, uncovered, for 2 minutes, stirring half way through the 2-minute time period. Mix in ¼ cup raisins and ½ cup diced reconstituted apples (steamed). Microwave on high for 2 minutes. Serve with spice cake or baked ham.

Apple Snax (16)

To make a crispy dried apple snack that can be flavored to taste like a strawberry, apricot, peach, or lime requires only a simple process and a little time.

Slice apples, pretreat by dipping in sodium bisulfite solution, sprinkle with flavored gelatin, or a diet flavored gelatin, and place in dehydrator to dry. After they are dry, place them on an ungreased cookie sheet and bake in the oven at 170° F. for 2 hours, or until crisp. They can also be spiced with cinnamon or cinnamon and sugar.

It is easier to treat the apples with gelatin while they are moist and before they are dried. However, by dipping the dried apples in water for 10 seconds they will absorb enough moisture to cause the gelatin to cling to the apple while it is being baked.

For a crisp apple without the extra calories, just bake the dried apple slices for 2 hours at 170° F.

Spiced Apple Yogurt (17)

To make spiced apple yogurt, blend ½ cup dehydrated apple slices with ½ cup water, ¼ teaspoon apple pie spice, and ¼ cup brown sugar. Blend to desired consistency—smooth or chunky. Stir into 2 cups plain chilled yogurt. For smooth yogurt, add the yogurt to the apples in the blender and puree until smooth. Return to the refrigerator to chill before using. This makes an excellent yogurt roll. Pour the chilled yogurt onto a teflex sheet and dry.

Applesauce Nut Squares (Microwave) (18)

- 1 cube margarine
- ⅓ cup granulated sugar
- ⅓ cup brown sugar, packed
- ¼ cup rehydrated applesauce*
- 1 cup sifted flour
- 1 tsp baking powder
- ¼ tsp cinnamon
- 1 egg
- 1 tsp vanilla
- ¼ cup chopped nuts
- ¼ cup raisins

Place margarine in an 8×8×2-inch glass baking dish and melt uncovered on high for 45 seconds. In mixer bowl place sugars and applesauce. Add melted margarine and blend well. Stir in flour, baking powder and cinnamon. Add egg and vanilla. Beat well. Add nuts and raisins. Stir lightly to combine. Cook uncovered on high for 4 minutes. Turn dish. Continue to cook for 1½ minutes. Cool and cut into squares.

*Measure ¼ cup apple slices into a measure, cover with boiling water to the ¼-cup level. Let stand for 5 minutes and puree in blender. Add a dash of apple pie spice and 1 teaspoon sugar, if desired.

Apricots (General Instructions) (19)

One of the favorite dried fruits available, but one of the hardest fruits to dry to perfection, is the apricot. When the apricot is dried, it is supposed to be soft, sweet, pliable and a beautiful orange color. It is almost impossible to buy a fresh orange apricot because food handlers forego flavor, color and sweetness in favor of firm, underripe fruit for ease of handling during transportation and for processing when it reaches its destination.

The first step in successfully drying apricots is to grow your own or make friends with the owner of an apricot orchard. Pick apricots when they are a beautiful orange color, full of flavor, sweet and just slightly pliable.

For those people who like firm yellow apricots, it is not necessary to pretreat. Just cut the apricots, remove pits, place in dehydrator and dry. If each half is cut into 2 slices, instead of being ¾-inch thick, they will be only 3/8-inch thick; and therefore will dry faster. Cut the apricot in half and remove the pit. Slice each half from top to bottom, parallel to the first cut.

Most people agree that the most flavorful apricot is one that is orange, soft, and juicy. To try to dry an apricot when it is at its peak for flavor is hard because the browning enzyme has started to cause quality loss in the apricot. To maintain a pretty color and have flavor it is necessary to stop that enzyme action. The best way to do that is by pretreating with sulfur. Sulfuring raises the temperature high enough to inactivate the browning enzyme but does not give a cooked taste. Sulfur also bleaches bruised spots and helps retain nutrients. For sulfuring and drying in the sun, instructions are available from the nearest Extension Service Office. *The ABC's of Home Food Dehydration* gives directions for sulfuring when drying in an electric dehydrator. Sun drying and dehydrator drying differ in the amount of sulfur used and also the time required in the sulfuring box. For the electric dehydrator, use one-half teaspoon of flowers of sulfur per pound of cut fruit, and leave in the sulfuring box just until all sulfur is burned (approximately 1 hour). Transfer the fruit to the dehydrator trays, place in the dehydrator, and dry. Place the dehydrator outside to prevent sulfur fumes from permeating the house.

It is possible to pretreat apricots by steaming. While the color is pretty, the apricot texture changes. It becomes tough, chewy, and tastes cooked instead of dried.

Sodium bisulfite bleaches, helps preserve the color of the flesh and helps retain natural Vitamin C; but will not penetrate the skin and protect the skin's color. In testing, apricots have been pretreated by soaking in sodium bisulfite from 2 minutes to 6 hours with the same end result. The flesh of the apricot has a good color but the skin is brown. With longer soaking, more moisture is absorbed, the drying time is lengthened, and there is loss of water soluable vitamins and minerals. Therefore, pretreat for 2 minutes only.

Each person must decide if pretreatment is necessary, and if so, which method of pretreatment will produce the quality desired in the product.

Apricot Acorns (20)

- 1 cup almond paste, crumbled
- ½ cup wheat germ
- 1 cup honey
- ½ cup sesame seeds
- 2 cups instant nonfat dry powdered milk
- 36 dried apricots (steamed)
- 36 whole cloves

In a bowl mix almond paste, wheat germ, honey, sesame seeds and powdered milk until the mixture is smooth and thoroughly combined. Shape mixture into 36 balls. Place apricot half on one side of each ball. Fasten apricot in place with a whole clove. Pinch the other side of the ball into a point to resemble an acorn. Place acorns side by side in a single layer on wax paper or foil and let dry at room temperature. Store in an air-tight container in a cool dry place until ready to serve.

Apricot-Almond Jam (21)

- 2 cups dried apricot halves
- 1 can (1 lb, 4 oz) crushed pineapple
- 6 cups sugar (approximately)
- 1 cup drained, canned pitted dark sweet cherries, halved
- ½ cup slivered almonds, toasted

Cut apricots into small pieces. Place in large saucepan; cover with water and soak about 6 hours. If necessary, add a little more water to cover fruit. Simmer 20 minutes. Add pineapple and liquid. Measure and add 1 cup sugar for each cup of fruit and liquid. Stir until sugar is dissolved, then simmer 20 minutes longer. Stir in cherries and remove from heat. When lukewarm, add almonds. Cool, then spoon into jars. Cover with lids and store in refrigerator. Makes about 4 pints.

Apricot Balls (22)

- 1½ cups dried apricots, ground or finely chopped
- ⅔ cup sweetened condensed milk (see recipe #164)
- 2 cups shredded coconut
- ½ cup ground almonds or walnuts
- Powdered sugar

Place all ingredients except powdered sugar into a bowl; mix well. Form into small balls and roll in powdered sugar. Let stand 1 hour and again roll in powdered sugar. Can be served at this point or stored in an airtight container. Can be frozen. For variation, use toasted coconut. Makes 3 dozen balls.

Apricot Bars (23)

- 1 cup dried apricots
- ¾ cup water
- 1 cup flour
- ¾ cube margarine
- 1½ cups brown sugar, firmly packed
- 1 Tbsp cornstarch
- ¼ tsp salt
- 2 tsp grated orange peel
- 2 Tbsp orange juice
- 2 eggs beaten
- 1½ cups coconut

Cut apricots in small pieces; combine with water; cover and simmer for 20 minutes. Meanwhile, mix flour, margarine, and ½ cup sugar; press crumbly mixture into greased 11 × 7-inch pan. Bake at 350° F. for 20 minutes. Mix 1 cup sugar, cornstarch, and salt; stir into undrained apricots and cook until thickened, stirring constantly. Remove from heat; stir in remaining ingredients, reserving a little coconut. Spread apricot mixture over baked crust; sprinkle top with reserved coconut. Bake at 350° F. for 25 minutes. Cool in pan; cut into bars. Makes 30 bars.

Nancy's Apricot Bars (24)

- ¾ cup soft shortening (part butter)
- 1 cup brown sugar, packed
- ¾ cup sifted flour
- ½ tsp soda
- 1 tsp salt
- 1½ cups rolled oats

Mix thoroughly. Place ½ mixture in greased 9 × 13-inch pan. Press and flatten. Spread with cooled filling* and cover with remaining crumb mixture. Bake until browned. Glaze** and cut into bars. Bake at 400° F. for 25-30 minutes.

Filling

- 3 cups dried apricot slices
- 1 cup dates cut up
- 1½ cups water
- ½ cup sugar

Pour boiling water over apricot slices and let stand for 5 minutes. Place in blender and puree until smooth. Add dates and ½ cup sugar. Spread over dough mixture.

****Glaze***

- ½ cup orange juice
- ¾ cup powdered sugar
- ½ tsp grated orange peel

Glaze and cut into bars. Makes 18-21 bars.

Apricot-Carrot Salad (25)

Steam ½ cup dehydrated chopped apricots until tender. Add 2 cups boiling water to a 6-ounce package of apricot jello. Stir until dissolved.

Add the chopped apricots, ½ cup dehydrated grated carrots, ½ cup raisins, and 2 cups of cold water. When it begins to thicken stir to evenly distribute the fruit throughout the salad and chill until set. Makes 10 servings.

If the carrots are not reconstituted by steaming, it is better to let the salad stand overnight to make a more tender carrot.

Apricot-Date Mini Rolls (26)

- ½ cup margarine
- 1 cup steamed apricot pieces, cut
- 1 cup chopped dates
- 8 oz miniature marshmallows
- 1 cup chopped nuts
- 2 cups graham cracker crumbs
- 1 tsp vanilla

Melt margarine and marshmallows together. Combine with other ingredients and mix well. Using half of the mixture, form into rolls about 2 inches in diameter and 18 inches long. Slice with a sharp knife into ½-inch pieces. Form the second half of the mixture into a long roll and slice also. Place on dehydrator trays and dry about 15 minutes or just until crunchy on the outside but still moist on the inside.

If you have a microwave oven, it takes only 2 minutes to heat the margarine and marshmallows using the high setting.

Apricot Hors d'oeuvres (27)

Chop ½ cup pecans, almonds or walnuts. Soften 6 ounces of cream cheese and blend in nuts. It may be necessary to add a little milk to get a good spreading consistency. Steam apricot or prune halves until they are soft and pliable. Fill with cheese and nut mixture.

Caution: Do not fill in advance because the dehydrated fruit has a tendency to draw moisture from the cheese.

Frosted Apricot Milk (28)

- 1 cup steamed apricot halves
- 1 tsp lemon juice
- 1 cup cold water
- 3 cups milk
- 1 pt vanilla ice cream

Puree apricot halves, water and lemon juice in blender. Add ½ cup milk and 1 scoop ice cream; blend thoroughly. Add remaining milk and mix well. Pour into tall glasses and top each with a scoop of ice cream.

Apricot Nut Bread (29)

- ¾ cup boiling water
- 1 cup dried apricots, chopped
- 1 Tbsp baking powder
- 2 eggs
- 1 cup chopped nuts
- ⅓ cup softened butter
- 3 cups flour
- ½ tsp salt
- 1 cup sugar
- ½ cup light corn syrup

Grease and lightly flour 9 x 5 x 3-inch loaf pan. Pour water over apricots; let stand 15 minutes. Mix together flour, baking powder and salt. Blend butter, sugar, eggs and corn syrup; mix until smooth and well blended. Stir in apricots with water in which they were soaked and stir in nuts. Add dry ingredients gradually. Spoon into prepared pan. Bake at 350° F. for 1 hour and 15 minutes or until cake tester inserted in center of the loaf comes out clean. Cool in pan 10 minutes. Remove from pan and cool on rack.

Apricot Penuche (30)

- 1 cup granulated sugar
- 1½ cups light brown sugar, packed
- ⅓ cup condensed milk
- ⅓ cup milk
- 2 Tbsp margarine
- 1 tsp vanilla
- ⅓ cup finely chopped dried apricots, reconstituted by steaming until soft
- ⅓ cup finely chopped almonds

Butter an 8 x 8-inch pan; set aside. In a 2-quart pan combine sugars, cream, milks, and margarine; stir until it is well mixed. Cook over medium heat, stirring constantly, until sugars dissolve and mixture begins to boil. Cook until mixture reaches 238° F. on candy thermometer. Remove pan from heat; cool mixture to 110° F. without stirring. Add vanilla to cooled mixture. Beat vigorously until candy thickens and starts to lose its gloss. Quickly stir in the apricots and nuts; spread evenly in the pan. Cut when cool and firm. Serve.

This candy is also good made with peaches. Be sure to reconstitute the peaches until they are soft, by steaming, or they will cause the penuche to set up too hard.

Apricot Squares (31)

- 1 cup chopped dried apricots
- 1 tsp lemon juice
- 5 cups Instant Cookie Mix*
- ¼ cup sugar
- 1 cup water
- ¼ cup water

Combine apricots, sugar, lemon juice and 1 cup water in saucepan. Cook over medium heat until thick, stirring frequently. Cool. Thoroughly combine cookie mix and ¼ cup water. Firmly pack half of mixture into a well-greased 8-inch square baking pan. Spread with apricot filling. Lightly pack remaining oatmeal mixture on top. Bake at 350° F. for 30 to 35 miniutes. Cool; cut into squares. Serves 16.

***Instant Cookie Mix**

- 2½ cups sifted flour
- 1¼ tsp salt
- 1 tsp soda
- 1 cup brown sugar, packed
- 1 cup granulated sugar
- 1½ cups shortening
- 3½ cups oatmeal, quick or old-fashioned

Sift together flour, salt and soda. Stir in sugars. Cut in shortening until mixture resembles coarse crumbs. Stir in oatmeal, mixing thoroughly. Store in covered container in refrigerator.

Stewed Apricots (Microwave) **(32)**

- 1 cup dried apricots
- 1 cup water
- 2 Tbsp sugar

Put ingredients into a 1½-quart glass casserole. Cook in microwave on high, covered, for 10 minutes. Let stand, covered, for 30 minutes. Refrigerate covered.

Use this method to prepare any dried stewed fruit separately or together. It may be necessary to change the amount of sugar.

Tip: To plump dried fruits in the microwave, place the fruit in a microwave-safe dish, add ¼ cup water per cup of dried fruit, cover with wax paper. Cook in microwave on high for 3 or 4 minutes, until it is moist. It is then ready to use in cakes, cookies or candies.

Baked Stuffed Apricots (Microwave) **(33)**

- 12 lrg dehydrated apricot halves reconstituted by steaming until tender
- ½ cup orange marmalade
- ½ cup chopped nuts

Place apricot halves, cut side up, in an 8-inch round baking dish. Fill each half with marmalade; sprinkle with nuts. Cover with plastic wrap and cook 4 minutes. Turn dish, cook 2 to 3 minutes longer. Serve warm or cold. Serves 6.

Apricot Taskets (34)

- 1¼ cups dried apricots
- 1 cup water
- 2 Tbsp sugar
- ½ tsp lemon juice
- 1 cup sifted flour
- ¼ cup sugar
- ¼ tsp salt
- ½ cup margarine
- 1 cup quick rolled oats, uncooked
- 5 Tbsp cold water

Combine apricots, 1 cup water, 2 tablespoons sugar and the lemon juice; place in medium-sized saucepan. Cook over low heat, stirring occasionally until thickened; cool.

Sift together flour, ¼ cup sugar and the salt into bowl. Cut in margarine until mixture resembles coarse crumbs. Stir in oats. Sprinkle water by tablespoonfuls over mixture. Stir lightly with fork until just dampened. If necessary, add another tablespoon of cold water to make the dough hold together. Form into ball. Divide dough in half. Roll each half on lightly-floured board or canvas to form a 9-inch square. Cut each half into nine 3-inch squares.

Place about 1 tablespoon filling diagonally across center of each square. Bring two opposite corners together. Press to seal. Bake on ungreased cookie sheets at 375° F. for 12 to 15 minutes or until delicately browned. Sprinkle with powdered sugar while warm. Makes 18.

Apricot-Chocolate Torte (35)

- 2 cups dried apricot halves reconstituted in 1 cup boiling water
- 2¼ cups flour
- 1 tsp soda
- ¾ tsp salt
- ¾ cup softened butter
- 1¾ cups sugar
- 1 tsp vanilla
- 3 eggs
- 1 6-oz package semisweet chocolate chips
- ¼ cup water
- Cream Topping*

In small bowl, combine flour, soda and salt; set aside. In large bowl, combine butter, sugar and vanilla; beat until creamy. Add eggs, one at a time, beating well after each addition. Blend in chocolate mixture (melt chips and water in microwave on simmer for 1 minute). Gradually add flour mixture alternately with juice from apricots. Pour into two greased and floured 9-inch round cake pans. Bake at 375° F. for 35 minutes or until the layers test done. Cool 10 minutes; remove from pans. Cool completely.

***Cream Topping**

- 2 cups heavy cream
- 2 Tbsp powdered sugar

In small bowl, beat cream and powdered sugar until stiff. Reserve 1 cup for top; fold chopped apricots into remaining whipped cream. Split cake layers and fill each with 1 cup apricot-cream mixture. Spread 1 cup reserved plain whipped cream over top of torte; garnish with slivered almonds. Makes 1 (9-inch) 4-layer torte.

Asparagus Soup (36)

- ½ cup dehydrated tomatoes
- 2 cups dehydrated asparagus
- 2 cups boiling water
- ⅛ tsp white pepper
- ½ tsp basil
- 1 Tbsp flour
- 2 cups water
- 2 tsp chicken base
- ¼ cup sour cream
- Salt to taste

In microwave oven place 2 cups of water and 2 teaspoons of chicken base. Heat to boiling. In blender combine remaining ingredients, except sour cream, and puree. Combine puree and chicken stock. Cook and stir until smooth and thickened. Fold in sour cream. Add salt to taste. Thin with half-and-half cream if desired. Serve hot with Cheese Squares. Serves 4.

Cheese Squares (37)

- 1 large loaf white bread, unsliced
- 1 cube butter, softened
- Pinch garlic salt
- ½ lb finely-shredded sharp cheese
- 3 egg whites
- Paprika

Trim the crust from the bread and cut in 1½-inch cubes. Combine butter, garlic salt and cheese. Beat until well mixed and fluffy. Beat egg whites until stiff and fold into cheese mixture. Spread on bread cubes on all but bottom side. Place on greased cookie sheet. Sprinkle with a little paprika on top. Bake 10 to 12 minutes at 350° F. Cheese squares should be puffed but not brown.

Baby Foods (General Instructions) (38)

Using dehydrated foods to make baby food is a real money saver. With a blender and some dehydrated food, baby can have a nutritious food experience. Be sure to check with baby's doctor to determine the age to begin introduction of solid foods.

Fruits with seeds, such as raspberries, strawberries and boysenberries should be pureed and strained before serving to small children.

For ease in blending foods, place 4 apricot halves in ⅓ cup water, simmer until soft, and puree. This can then be diluted with formula or milk (depending on age) and served. Remember, dehydrated food is concentrated. Even though this is a small amount, it is the same as 2 fresh apricots. When feeding baby, this is important to remember.

Any fruit can be prepared in the above manner. Fruits can be added to milk puddings or cereal.

Vegetables can be prepared in the same way as fruits. Place ¼ cup of any vegetable in ⅓ cup of water, simmer until soft, and puree. Add more water to dilute or add formula for a creamed vegetable. Some vegetables may need to be strained to remove fibers, such as celery. Meat can also be pureed and added to the vegetable or served separately.

As the baby gets older, instead of making a puree, chop the fruits and vegetables and have "junior foods."

Any of the soup recipes can be used if baby's portion is removed before seasoning.

Bananas (General Instructions) (39)

The banana chip that is purchased in markets is a freeze dried Plantain banana that is very starchy. It is pretreated in an invert sugar, banana oil solution and dried. Plantains are used in South and Central America much like potatoes are used in the United States—baked, fried, etc. Because of the starch content they are more crisp when dried.

To get a more crisp banana chip from the local bananas available in the produce stands (Chiquita and Dole), cut the slices about ⅛-inch thick and pretreat them in a sodium bisulfite solution. To make them very crisp, place the dehydrated bananas on an ungreased cookie sheet and bake at 170° F. for 2 hours. To maintain crispness, store in a jar with a tight-fitting lid. This is most important in areas with high humidity.

Banana Teethers (40)

Peel and cut banana lengthwise in eights. It is easier to cut the banana in half lengthwise and then cut each half in four strips. Dip strips in sodium bisulfite solution for 2 minutes and dehydrate. The strips are easier for the baby to hold than slices are, and the sodium bisulfite treatment helps keep a pleasing color. For a more crisp teether, bake at 170° F. for 2 hours. Store in covered jar to maintain crispness.

Banana Bars (41)

- ¼ cup butter
- 1 cup sugar
- 2 eggs
- 2 cups flour
- 2 tsp baking powder
- ½ tsp salt
- 1 cup banana leather pieces
- ½ tsp lemon extract
- ½ tsp vanilla extract

Reconstitute bananas by breaking leather into pieces. Place in the blender and add boiling water to the 1-cup measure. Puree until smooth.

In mixer bowl, cream together butter, sugar; add eggs and beat well. Sift together flour, baking powder and salt. Add the flour mixture alternately with the banana mixture to the creamed mixture. Add lemon and vanilla extract. Mix well. Spread into greased 9 x 13-inch pan. Bake at 350° F. for 30 minutes. While still warm, frost with lemon frosting. When cool, cut into bars.

Lemon Frosting (42)

- 2 cups powdered sugar
- ½ square margarine
- 2 Tbsp lemon juice
- 1 Tbsp lemon rind

Mix well and spread on bars.

Banana-Date Scones (43)

- 2 cups flour
- 1 Tbsp date sugar (recipe #97)
- ½ tsp baking powder
- 1 tsp salt
- ¼ cup margarine
- 2 eggs
- ¼ cup whipping cream
- 1¾ cups dehydrated banana leather reconstituted
- ¾ cup chopped dates

To reconstitute bananas, place 1¾ cups banana leather in the blender. Add boiling water to the 1¾-cup measure and puree until smooth.

In bowl, stir together flour, sugar, baking powder and salt. Cut in margarine until mixture crumbles. Beat eggs, reserve 2 tablespoons of the egg mixture. Add cream and reconstituted mashed banana to the remaining egg. Add this and dates to flour mixture, stirring gently until all is moistened. Place on lightly-floured board, and pat to ½-inch thickness. Cut into diamond shapes and place on lightly-greased baking sheets. Brush tops with egg and sprinkle with sugar. Bake at 450° F. for 15 minutes.

Banana Nut Bread (44)

- ½ cup shortening
- 1 cup brown sugar
- 2 eggs
- ½ of a 2-cup banana roll
- 2 cups sifted flour
- 1 tsp soda
- ½ tsp salt
- ½ cup nuts

Break one cup of banana roll into pieces and place in blender. Add enough water to make 1 cup. Let stand while collecting other ingredients. Puree banana roll and water to a smooth consistency and add other ingredients. Add the nuts at end of blending time so they do not get pureed. Pour into a well-greased bread pan and bake for 1 hour at 350° F.

Banana Streusel Coffee Cake (45)

- 1 cup banana leather reconstituted by adding boiling water to the 1-cup measure.
- ½ cup sour cream
- 1 tsp vanilla
- ⅓ cup soft butter or margarine
- ⅔ cup packed brown sugar
- 2 eggs
- 2½ cups flour
- 2¼ tsp baking powder
- 1 tsp soda
- ½ tsp salt
- ½ tsp cinnamon
- ¼ tsp nutmeg
- Streusel Filling

In blender, mix banana and water. Puree until smooth. Add sour cream and vanilla. Set aside. In large bowl, cream butter and brown sugar. Beat in eggs one at a time. Mix dry ingredients; blend into sugar mixture alternately with banana mixture. Pour half of batter into a greased 9-inch tube pan or 9×5×3-inch loaf pan; sprinkle with Streusel Filling.* Pour remaining batter into pan over filling. Bake at 350° F. for 55 to 60 minutes, until cake tests done. Serves 12.

Streusel Filling

- 2 Tbsp flour
- 2 Tbsp sugar
- 1 Tbsp cocoa
- ½ tsp cinnamon
- 2 Tbsp soft butter or margarine
- ¼ cup chopped nuts

Mix all ingredients in a small bowl.

Beef Country Pie (46)

Crust

- ½ cup rehydrated tomato sauce
- ½ cup bread crumbs
- 1 lb ground beef
- 1 Tbsp dehydrated onion, chopped
- 1 Tbsp chopped dehydrated green pepper
- 1½ tsp salt
- ⅛ tsp oregano
- ⅛ tsp pepper

Combine these ingredients and mix well. Pat meat mixture into the bottom and pinch 1-inch flutings around the edges of a greased 9-inch pie plate. Set aside.

Filling

- 1⅓ cups brown minute rice (See recipe #238)
- 1 cup water
- 1 cup rehydrated tomato sauce
- ½ tsp salt
- 1 cup grated Cheddar cheese

Pour 1 cup of boiling water over brown rice and let stand for 10 minutes. Add tomato sauce, salt and ¼ cup of the cheese. Spoon rice mixture into meat shell. Cover with aluminum foil. Bake at 350° F. for 25 minutes. Uncover and sprinkle top with remaining cheese. Return to oven and bake uncovered 10 minutes longer. Cut into pie-shaped pieces. Serves 6.

Blueberry Kuchen (47)

- 1 pkg white cake mix
- 2 cups blueberry pie filling*
- ¼ cup sugar
- ½ cup margarine
- 1 cup sour cream
- 1 egg, beaten

Crumble cake mix and margarine together until mixture resembles coarse corn meal. Pat mixture into a 13 × 9 × 2-inch pan. Bake at 350° F. for 15 minutes or until lightly brown. Cool. Spread blueberry filling over cake. Mix sour cream, sugar and egg together. Spread over blueberry filling. Bake at 350° F. for 30 minutes or until topping is set.

****Blueberry Pie Filling***

Place 2½ cups dehydrated blueberries in pan, add 1¼ cups water and ⅓ cup sugar. Bring to a boil. Dissolve 1¼ tablespoons cornstarch in a small amount of water and stir into boiling berries. Cook, stirring continuously, until thickened and clear. Remove from heat, and cool.

Blueberry Pudding Cheesecake (48)

- 1 cup cream cheese
- 1 pkg Instant Lemon Pudding
- 2 cups milk
- 1 9-inch graham cracker crust

Stir cream cheese until very soft. Gradually blend in ½ cup of milk until smooth and creamy. Add remaining milk and pudding mix. Beat slowly with egg beater 1 minute. (Do not over-beat.) Pour into cool graham cracker crust. Garnish with Blueberries.

Place 2 cups dehydrated blueberries in pan and cover with 1 cup boiling water. Simmer for 10 minutes and add ⅓ cup of sugar. Dissolve 1 tablespoon cornstarch in a small amount of water and cook, stirring constantly, until thickened and clear. Cool. Spread on top center of cheesecake. Sprinkle graham cracker crumbs around outer edge. Chill and serve.

Borsht (Beet Soup) (49)

- 1 cup diced dehydrated beets reconstituted by adding boiling water to the 1-cup measure
- 1½ cups yogurt
- ½ tsp salt
- 1 Tbsp lemon juice
- ¼ tsp onion salt
- Yogurt for garnish

Place beets and boiling water in blender and puree until smooth. Cool. Add yogurt, salt, lemon juice and onion salt. Blend until well mixed. Serve chilled, with a dollop of yogurt on top. A very colorful soup. Serves 2.

Breakfast Delight (50)

- 1 ripe papaya
- 1 cup lemon flavored yogurt
- ¼ cup wheat germ

Cut papaya in half lengthwise. Scoop out and discard seeds. Fill hollows with mounds of lemon yogurt (see recipe #309) and top with wheat germ.

Breakfast Roll (51)

- ¼ cup dried egg product reconstituted in ⅓ cup water
- ½ cup powdered milk (do not add water)
- 1 tsp vanilla (optional)
- 3 oz frozen orange juice concentrate (do not add water)
- 1 cup fruit in season (strawberries, pineapple, bananas, etc.)

Place in blender and puree. Pour onto plastic wrap and dry. Sprinkle with coconut, nuts, or seeds if desired. Set the dehydrator for 145° F. It will take about 12 hours for this to dry. Remove from plastic wrap while still warm, roll in new wrap, and store in refrigerator. For camping it is permissible to leave the roll unrefrigerated for several days; however, do not store in direct sunlight, but keep in a cool place.

Boysenberry Breakfast Frappe (52)

- 1 cup dehydrated boysenberry leather (seeds strained before dehydrating)
- ½ cup milk
- 2 cups plain yogurt

Place all ingredients in blender. Puree until smooth. Garnish with fresh pineapple spear. Serves 4.

Any dehydrated fruit without seeds, or any leathers with seeds strained, will make inviting breakfast drinks.

Bread Crumbs (General Instructions) (53)

To make bread crumbs, place 1 loaf of bread in the dehydrator for one to two hours. When it is evenly dried, remove it from the dehydrator and place in a plastic bag and roll with a rolling pin to make fine crumbs. It can also be put in blender or food processor to make fine crumbs.

Cream of Broccoli Soup (54)

- 2 cups dehydrated broccoli pieces
- 2 cups boiling water
- 1 Tbsp dehydrated onion
- ¼ tsp pepper
- 1 can condensed chicken broth
- 2 Tbsp butter
- 2 Tbsp flour
- 1 tsp salt
- 2 cups half-and-half

Reconstitute broccoli pieces by blending with water until smooth. Add all ingredients except half-and-half. Puree until smooth. Heat half-and-half but do not boil. Add broccoli mixture to the half-and-half and heat. Add a dash of nutmeg if desired and serve.

Carrot Cake (55)

- ¾ cup butter or margarine
- ¼ cup granulated sugar
- 1 cup brown sugar
- 2 cups grated dehydrated carrots
- 2 eggs beaten
- ⅓ cup sour milk (⅓ cup milk plus 1 tsp vinegar)
- 2 cups flour
- 1 Tbsp baking powder
- ¼ tsp soda
- 1 tsp salt
- ½ tsp cinnamon
- ⅔ cup chopped pecans

Cream butter or margarine and sugars. Place 2 cups dehydrated grated carrots in blender and add water to the 2-cup measure. Puree until smooth. Add carrots and eggs to creamed mixture. Sift dry ingredients and mix with nuts. Add dry ingredients and milk alternately to creamed mixture. Pour into two greased and floured 8 or 9-inch cake pans. Bake at 350° F. for 35 minutes or until cake tests done. Cool and frost with cream cheese frosting.

Cream Cheese Frosting (56)

- ½ cup cream cheese
- 1½ tsp vanilla
- 3 cups sifted powdered sugar
- 6 Tbsp margarine
- 1 Tbsp milk

Cream cheese and butter. Add vanilla, milk and powdered sugar. Mix until smooth and of spreading consistency. Frost and serve.

Carrot Nut Bread (57)

- 1 cup shredded dehydrated carrot
- ½ cup corn oil
- ¾ cup sugar
- 2 eggs
- 1¾ cup flour
- 2½ tsp baking powder
- ½ tsp salt
- 1 tsp cinnamon
- ½ cup chopped nuts

In blender, place 1 cup shredded carrots and add water to the 1-cup measure. Let stand for a few minutes and then puree to smooth consistency. Add corn oil and sugar. Add eggs, one at a time, blending after each addition. Add remaining ingredients except nuts. Blend. Stir in nuts. Pour into a greased 8½ × 4½ × 2½-inch loaf pan. Bake at 350° F. for 55 to 60 minutes.

Carrot Soup (58)

- 4 cups dehydrated grated carrots
- 2 cups dehydrated potato slices
- 3 cups boiling water
- 1 small onion, grated
- 2 Tbsp margarine
- 4 cups well-flavored chicken broth or 4 Tbsp chicken base dissolved in 4 cups water
- Salt and pepper
- 1 cup milk

Combine carrots and potatoes with boiling water and let stand for 10 minutes. Saute onion in saucepan with margarine until limp. Add rehydrated vegetables and chicken broth. Simmer for 10 minutes. Season to taste. Puree ingredients in blender, return to pan, add milk, reheat slowly and serve.

Chilled Carrot Soup (59)

- 4 cups lightly-packed grated dehydrated carrots
- 2 cups boiling water
- 3 Tbsp margarine or butter
- ½ medium onion, chopped
- 3 Tbsp flour
- 2 chicken bouillon cubes
- 3 cups milk
- 1 tsp salt
- ⅛ tsp white pepper

Reconstitute dehydrated carrots in 2 cups boiling water. Puree in blender. Melt butter in heavy saucepan. Add onion and saute until tender but not brown. Blend in flour. Add bouillon cubes. Gradually stir in milk and cook, stirring, over moderate heat until soup thickens and just comes to a boil. Stir in seasonings and carrots. Chill several hours or overnight. Garnish with sprigs of parsley, chives, dill, sour cream, etc. Makes 6 cups.

Bakers' Cheese (60)

- 2 qts powdered nonfat milk (Mix as directed on pkg)
- 1 pt cultured buttermilk
- ½ tsp salt

To make cheese from pasteurized milk, it is necessary to use cultured buttermilk or rennet to activate the curdling process. Use stainless steel, enamel, or glazed crockery vessels. Combine milk and buttermilk in heavy 4-quart pan. Heat at medium until temperature reaches 170° F. Use a candy or deep-fat thermometer to check temperature. When milk reaches 170° F. reduce heat to low. In about 1 hour, thick white curds will separate from the whey. Line a colander with 2 or 3 thicknesses of cheesecloth wrung out of cold water. Gently spoon the curds into the colander. When most of the curds have been removed, pour remaining curds and whey through a fine stainless steel sieve. Add the curds to the colander and allow to drain for 1 hour. Scrape cheese into a bowl and mix in salt. Cover and keep in refrigerator. Makes about 2 cups.

Cream Cheese (61)

Follow directions in recipe #60 except use whole milk. To make it creamy, chill the whey and skim off butterlike cream and put it back into the curds. Place in blender and whip until smooth. Add salt and additional cream if desired. Store in refrigerator. The homemade cheese stays fresh up to about one week. The cheese can be frozen but should be completely thawed and whipped in an electric mixer on low speed to blend before using.

Ricotta Cheese (62)

- 2 quarts fresh pasteurized skim milk
- ½ cup strained fresh lemon juice or 3 Tbsp white vinegar
- Salt, optional

Combine milk and vinegar in stainless steel pan. Set over very low heat and bring slowly to a temperature of 200° F., just below the boiling point. Remove from heat, cover and place in unheated dehydrator to remain undisturbed about 6 hours or until solid curd forms. Line a colander with dampened cheese cloth; set it over a bowl. Turn the clabbered milk into the sieve and allow the whey to drain off until it reaches the desired ricotta texture. Salt, if desired, and store in refrigerator. Use within 4 or 5 days. For a richer ricotta, use whole milk and save the cream from the whey and add back to it. Excellent used in lasagna.

Cherries (General Instructions) (63)

The temperature for drying cherries is important. This is one fruit that cannot be rushed. The fruit tastes scorched if dried at too high a temperature. Set dehydrator at 130° F. and *do not use recycle* if your dehydrator is so equipped.

Cherry-Chocolate Snack Cake (64)

- 1⅔ cup flour
- 1 cup brown sugar, packed
- ¼ cup cocoa
- 1 tsp soda
- ½ tsp salt
- 1 cup water
- ⅓ cup oil
- 1 tsp vinegar
- ½ tsp vanilla
- ⅓ cup chopped unblanched almonds
- ½ cup cherries steamed and diced

Mix flour, brown sugar, cocoa, soda, salt, and almonds in 8 x 8 x 2-inch ungreased pan. Add water, oil, vinegar, vanilla and cherries, stirring with a fork until fairly well mixed. Bake at 350° F. 35-40 minutes. Dust with powdered sugar, if desired.

Applesauce Snack Cake (64A)

Omit cocoa and vanilla. Stir 1½ teaspoons allspice into the flour mixture. Reduce water to ½ cup and stir in ½ cup of reconstituted applesauce.

To make applesauce, place ½ cup apple slices in blender and add boiling water to the ½-cup measure. Puree until smooth. To make applesauce from leather, break ½ cup leather in pieces and add water to the ½ cup measure. Puree until smooth.

Pear Snack Cake (64B)

Omit cocoa and vanilla. Stir 1½ teaspoons cinnamon into the flour mixture. Reduce water to ½ cup and stir in ½ cup of reconstituted pear sauce. Make the same as apple sauce.

Pumpkin Snack Cake (64C)

Omit cocoa and vanilla. Stir 1½ teaspoons pumpkin pie spice into the flour mixture. Reduce water to ½ cup and stir in ½ cup of reconstituted pumpkin leather. Reconstitute following directions above.

Substitute any fruit to make this easy *Snack Cake.*

Cherry Cream Cheese Pie (65)

- 1 baked pastry shell (9 inch) cooled
- 1 cup cream cheese
- 1⅓ cup sweetened condensed milk (see recipe #164)
- ⅓ cup fresh or bottled lemon juice

Combine cheese, milk and juice and mix until well blended. Pour this mixture into a cooled pastry crust and refrigerate for 2-3 hours. Then top with blueberry, cherry, blackberry, boysenberry, raspberry or strawberry pie filling.

Cherry Pie Filling (65A)

- 2½ cups dehydrated pie cherries
- 1¼ cups water
- ½ cup sugar
- 1¼ Tbsp cornstarch
- ¼ tsp almond extract

Place cherries in pan, add water and sugar. Bring to a boil. Dissolve cornstarch in a small amount of water and stir into boiling cherries. Cook, stirring continuously, until thickened and clear. Remove from heat. Add almond extract, and cool. Place on top of pie.

Substitute any of the berries desired. Prepare in the same manner. A sweeter berry will only require ⅓ cup sugar. Change spice or flavoring as desired.

Cherry Nut Pudding Cake (Microwave) (66)

Cherry Pie Filling

- 2½ cups dehydrated pie cherries
- 1¼ cups water
- ½ cup sugar
- 1¼ Tbsp cornstarch

Reconstitute cherries in water, with sugar, and thicken with cornstarch dissolved in a small amount of cold water. Spread filling in a 8 × 11-inch utility dish.

- 1 9-oz pkg one-layer cake mix, white or yellow
- ½ cup butter or margarine, melted
- 1 cup chopped nuts

Sprinkle dry cake mix over pie filling. Drizzle melted butter over mixture. Sprinkle with nuts. Bake 16 minutes, covered with paper toweling, turning dish once.

For variety, use different fruits and adjust the amount of sugar according to the sweetness of the fruit chosen.

Cherry Pie Pan Cakes (67)

- 2 Tbsp margarine
- 2 Tbsp sugar
- 1 large egg
- ½ cup flour
- ⅛ tsp salt
- ⅓ cup milk

Cream margarine and sugar. Beat in egg. Fold in flour and salt. Gradually add milk.

Grease four 8-inch shallow pie plates. Warm in the oven before spooning batter into them. Bake 10 minutes on top rack of a 425° F. oven. Serve with Sour Cherry Puree.

Sour Cherry Puree (67A)

- 2½ cups pitted dehydrated sour cherries
- 1¼ cups boiling water
- ½ tsp almond extract
- ¼ tsp cinnamon
- ½ cup sugar
- 1¼ Tbsp cornstarch

Reconstitute cherries in boiling water. Puree in blender until smooth. Add almond extract, cinnamon and sugar. Thicken with cornstarch dissolved in a small amount of cold water. Bring pureed sauce to a boil, add cornstarch and cook, stirring constantly until thickened. *Caution:* Overbeating cornstarch-based sauces thins them.

Chicken-Noodle Soup (68)

- 2 cups dehydrated chicken cubes
- 2 cups boiling water to reconstitute above
- 1½ quarts of water
- 1 Tbsp dehydrated chopped onion
- ½ cup finely chopped dehydrated celery
- 1 tsp dried parsley
- 2 tsp salt
- ⅛ tsp pepper
- 1 tsp crushed rosemary
- 2 cups uncooked homemade noodles (see recipe #167)

Place all ingredients except noodles in a Dutch oven. Bring to a boil and simmer 30 minutes. Stir in noodles and simmer another 20 minutes, or until noodles are done. Serves 8.

Chicken, Noodles and Nectarines (69)

- 2 broiler-fryers, halved (about 2 lb each)
- ¼ cup catsup
- ¼ cup water
- ¼ cup melted butter
- ¼ cup apple juice
- 2 Tbsp tarragon vinegar
- 2 tsp soy sauce
- ½ lb spinach noodles
- 3 cups dehydrated nectarine slices reconstituted by steaming
- 1 can (5 oz) drained water chestnuts
- ½ cup chopped green onion
- Salt and pepper

Wash chicken; pat dry. Arrange in 13×9×2-inch baking pan. Mix catsup, water, butter, apple juice, vinegar and soy sauce; pour over chicken. Marinate several hours, turning often. Bake skin side down at 425° F. for 25 minutes, basting often with sauce. Turn and baste; bake 35 minutes longer until tender. Cook noodles as package directs (see recipe #167 for homemade noodles); drain. Spoon sauce from chicken over noodles; fold in nectarines, chestnuts, onion, salt and pepper. Heat through. Turn onto hot platter. Serve at once.

Baked Chicken with Rosemary (70)

- 6 split chicken breasts
- Salt and pepper
- Softened butter
- 1 tsp powdered rosemary

Lay chicken breasts in an 8×11-inch oblong baking dish. Cover bottom of dish with ½-inch of water. Season breasts with salt and pepper, spread butter over meat, and sprinkle with rosemary. Cover with foil and cook for 1½ hours at 350°F. Add more water if necessary to keep chicken moist. Remove foil and broil for the last 15 minutes of cooking time to brown chicken.

Chili Con Carne with Beans (71)

- 1 med onion coarsely chopped
- 1 clove garlic, mashed
- 2 Tbsp oil
- 1 lb ground beef
- 1 tsp dried parsley powdered
- 2 cups tomato slices reconstituted in 1 cup water Place in blender and chop
- 1 Tbsp chili powder
- 2 cups red kidney beans, cooked

Saute onion and garlic in oil until onion is soft. Add ground beef. Stir constantly, breaking it up into small pieces, until browned. Add the rest of the ingredients. Stir well and bring to a boil. Reduce heat and simmer slowly for 1 hour.

Citrus Fruit (72)

Do not rush out and buy a case of oranges to dry. They aren't that good. If you have an orange tree and the fruit will spoil if it isn't preserved—experiment. Valencia oranges are sweet and are recommended for freezing to make juice. Navel oranges have a tendency to bitterness if frozen. There hasn't been much experimentation with dehydration.

Citrus fruits, washed and sliced in 3/8-inch circles and dried can be used to garnish punch bowls and they also add flavor.

Orange slices can be cut in half and used as a snack food.

Try orange tapioca leather. Sprinkle 1 tablespoon of minute tapioca over 1 cup fresh orange juice. Cook the tapioca and juice only to the boiling point, do not boil. Remove from heat and let it stand for 3 minutes. Stir, and let it stand for 3 more minutes. Stir and cool. Cool for 10 minutes undisturbed and then pour onto teflex sheet and dry.

Citrus Peel (General Instructions) (73)

Grapefruit Peel—With a sharp knife, slice a thick layer off top and bottom of the grapefruit after it has been washed thoroughly. Score peel into quarters. Remove sections with fingers. Cover peel with water in a saucepan (½ teaspoon salt to one quart water) and bring to a boil. Drain. Repeat process with salted water 3 more times. Using the tip of a spoon, scrape most of the white membrane from the peel. Cut into strips ¼-inch wide. For a more bitter peel do not remove so much of the white membrane. Place in dehydrator at 120°F. until dry. Store in strips until ready to use. Remember, dehydrated peel is concentrated, so use only half as much as required in recipes calling for fresh peel.

All citrus peels should be prepared in the same manner as grapefruit. Wash to remove dirt, wax or chemicals. The outer part of the peel contains the flavoring oils and the white membrane is what makes the peel bitter. Because of the oil concentration in the skin, citrus rinds provide more flavor than the juice. To prevent loss of flavoring oils, do not grate the peel until needed.

Bright Holiday Candied Peel (Grapefruit) (74)

- 1½ oz lime or strawberry-flavored gelatin
- ½ cup water
- ½ cup sugar
- 1 cup grapefruit strips

Combine gelatin, water and sugar in heavy saucepan. Add grapefruit strips and bring to a boil. Reduce heat and continue cooking over medium heat, stirring occasionally until peel is translucent and almost all of the syrup has been absorbed. Drain. Toss drained peel in granulated sugar. Spread out on teflex sheet to dry. Store in tightly-covered container. Set dehydrator at 120° F.

Candied Citrus Peel (75)

- 1 cup lemon, lime, orange or grapefruit peel
- ¼ cup water
- 1 cup sugar

Bring ¼ cup water and ½ cup sugar to boiling point. Reduce heat, add peel, and simmer 10 minutes. Remove from heat and let stand 12 hours. Using slotted spoon, carefully remove peel and add ½ cup sugar to syrup and bring to a boil. Carefully add peel and continue to simmer until most of the syrup has been absorbed and the peel is translucent. Watch carefully so it doesn't scorch. Drain. Sprinkle granulated sugar on a tray and coat peel. Place on dehydrator tray and dry at 120° F. Store in tightly covered container.

Citrus Flavored Sugars (General Instructions) (76)

Remove the colored part of the rind from lemon, lime, tangerine and orange fruits and place on top of ¾ cup of sugar in a bowl with a tight-fitting lid. Store covered in a cool place. Use this sugar to sweeten citrus flavored yogurts. It can also be used to add zest to custards. Remove the strips of peel and use only the sugar.

Citrus Zests (General Instructions) (77)

Citrus rinds have a stronger flavor than juice because of the heavy oil concentration in the colored portion of the skin. The white membrane is bitter, so be careful to not grate too deeply into the rind. There is a special tool available from gourmet shops that can be used to thinly peel just the outer part of the skin. It is called a "zester." This outer layer can also be removed with a sharp knife or a potato peeler.

Coconut (General Instructions) (78)

Remove coconut shell, pare the brown skin away with a vegetable parer. Grate the coconut, using the medium grating disc. Place on teflex sheet, set dehydrator at 130° F. and dry. Watch the coconut closely and remove a piece to cool before testing for dryness. When it is warm it doesn't appear to be dry, but when it cools it is sometimes too dry. It will take only 1 or 2 hours depending on the drying conditions for the day.

Coconut can be pared into thin slices to be used in trail mix.

Coconut Chocolate Cake (79)

- 2¼ cups sifted flour
- 2 cups sugar
- ½ cup shortening
- 1 tsp salt
- 3 squares melted chocolate
- ¾ cup milk

Combine above ingredients and beat for 2 minutes in mixer. Add

- 1½ tsp soda
- ½ tsp baking powder
- 3 eggs
- ½ cup milk
- 1 tsp vanilla

Mix thoroughly. Pour into two 9-inch layer pans which have been generously greased and floured. Bake at 350° F. for 40 minutes. Cool cakes in pan for 10 minutes. Before removing, loosen edges from pan with spatula. Place rack over cake and pan; invert together.

Fluffy White Icing (79A)

- 1½ cups sugar
- ⅛ tsp cream of tartar
- ⅓ cup water
- 2 egg whites, unbeaten
- 1 tsp vanilla
- ¾ cup dehydrated coconut

Place sugar, cream of tartar, water and egg whites in top of double boiler. Cook over boiling water, beating constantly with a beater until icing stands in peaks (about 7 minutes). Stir in vanilla. Spread between layers, on top and sides of cake. Cover cake with coconut. Sprinkle with chocolate chips.

Coconut Mousse (80)

- 1 qt milk
- 1½ cups sugar
- ¼ tsp salt
- 1 tsp almond extract
- 2 cups dehydrated grated coconut (see recipe #78)
- 4 Tbsp unflavored gelatin
- ½ cup cold water
- 5 egg whites, stiffly beaten
- 1 pt whipped cream

Bring milk to a boil. Add sugar, salt, almond extract and coconut. Soften gelatin in cold water. Heat, stirring constantly until gelatin is dissolved. Add to milk mixture. Chill until slightly thickened. Fold in egg whites and whipped cream. Pour into oiled 12-cup mold. Chill until firm. Serve with Carmel Sauce.

Carmel Sauce (80A)

- 1 Tbsp butter
- 2¼ cups packed brown sugar
- 2 egg yolks
- 1 cup cream
- 1 Tbsp vanilla
- ½ cup toasted slivered, blanched almonds
- ⅛ tsp salt

Mix in top of double boiler until creamy. When sauce is smooth, add almonds. Makes 3 cups of sauce.

Corn (General Instructions) (81)

Everyone likes juicy, sweet corn. Remember the story about harvesting corn—put the pot of water on to boil, go to the patch, pick the corn and run, don't walk, to the house to plunge it into boiling water so it will not turn to starch.

Well, a university has developed a new corn, Ilini Xtra-Sweet, which does not turn to starch for 24 hours. Sounds great—no more pretreatment of corn required because in 24 hours it is all dried and stored and it should be sweet. *Fact:* It may not turn to starch but there is still some enzyme action that causes flavor loss if corn is not pretreated by steaming before it is dehydrated.

In an experiment, corn was picked fresh. The kernels were cut off from several cobs and placed in the dehydrator to dry. Several cobs were steam blanched, cooled, the kernels were cut off, and they were placed in the dehydrator and dried. The sample trays were dried in the same dehydrator at the same temperature under the same conditions, the only exception being the pretreatment by steaming. Then the corn was reconstituted and served to a test group of 15 people. All 15 agreed that the pretreated corn had a better flavor. Should corn be pretreated? The best way to determine which method is best is to try both ways and decide after tasting.

In the recipes in this book, *dehydrated corn* refers to corn that has been cut off from the cob and dehydrated. *Dried corn* refers to whole kernel corn that has been sun dried and contains fiber. Dried corn makes excellent cornmeal, but it is tough and hard to reconstitute for use as a vegetable. If dehydrated corn is used to make cornmeal, it requires more moisture and some flour to be added to the recipe.

Corn-Cheese Souffle (82)

- 1¾ cups dehydrated corn
- 1 cup milk
- 1 Tbsp butter or margarine
- ¾ cup grated process American cheese
- 3 eggs, separated
- 1 Tbsp sugar
- ¼ tsp salt

Simmer corn in 1 cup water for 10 minutes; cool slightly and place in blender and chop. Add milk, return to pan, and continue cooking for 10 minutes. Remove from heat and stir in butter and cheese until both are melted. Slowly add beaten egg yolks, then add sugar and salt. Beat egg whites until stiff, but not dry, and fold into corn mixture. Pour into a lightly greased 2-quart casserole. Bake at 350° F. for 35 minutes. Serves 8.

Corn Chowder (83)

- ¼ cup margarine
- ½ cup finely-chopped onion
- ½ cup finely chopped green pepper
- 2 qts milk
- 2 cups dehydrated corn
- ⅓ cup cornstarch
- 4 strips bacon, cooked and crumbled
- 2 tsp salt
- 1 tsp sugar
- ¼ tsp pepper

In skillet, melt margarine; saute onion over medium heat until transparent. Add green pepper; saute until tender.

In a 3-quart saucepan, stir together 1½ quarts of the milk and the corn. Bring to a boil over medium heat. Reduce heat and simmer 15 minutes. Add cornstarch to remaining 2 cups of milk and stir until smooth. Add to corn mixture. Stir in bacon, salt, sugar, pepper, sauteed onion and green pepper. Bring to a boil and boil 1 minute, stirring constantly.

For those who do not like the chewiness of the corn, it is possible to chop the corn and 2 cups of milk in the blender before boiling it.

Indian Corn (84)

- 3 qts popped corn
- 1 cup monukka raisins
- 1 cup steamed, finely cut dried apricots
- 1 cup firmly packed light brown sugar
- 1 cup light corn syrup
- ⅓ cup evaporated milk
- 1 Tbsp butter
- ⅛ tsp salt
- 12 to 14 wooden skewers

In a large shallow pan mix popped corn, raisins and apricots. In a 2-quart saucepan mix sugar, corn syrup, evaporated milk, butter and salt. Stir over low heat until the sugar is dissolved. Increase heat to medium; continue cooking and stirring 15 minutes (234° F. if using a candy thermometer). Pour over the corn mixture; with two forks mix lightly to coat well; cool 5 minutes. Coat palms of hands lightly with butter, then shape mixture into ears; cool on wax paper. When cool, push skewer into one end of each ear.

Kenny's Corn Pudding (85)

- 1 cup dehydrated corn reconstituted in 2 cups water
- 2 eggs
- 1 cup evaporated milk
- 1 tsp salt
- 1/8 tsp white pepper
- 1 Tbsp melted butter

Place all ingredients in a blender. Blend until the ingredients are well blended, but not completely pureed. Pour the corn mixture into a well-greased 1-quart baking dish; place in a shallow pan of water, and bake at 350° F. for 50 minutes. For a brown crust, remove the dish from the water for the last 15 minutes of baking time. The pudding is done when the center is firm.

Dehydrated Corn Soup (86)

- 2 cups dehydrated corn
- 1 small onion, diced
- 2 cups water
- 1 Tbsp flour
- 1 qt milk
- 4 Tbsp butter
- Salt and pepper

Combine the corn, onion and water and cook for 10 minutes, stirring constantly to keep it from sticking to the pan. Place in blender and puree until smooth. Blend the flour to a smooth cream with 3-4 tablespoons cold milk. Pour the rest of the milk into a saucepan and bring just to a boil. Add the flour-cream to the milk, stirring briskly all the time. Cook over a low heat until the sauce comes to a boil and thickens. Stir continuously to prevent lumps from forming. Add the butter and simmer very gently for 3 minutes so that the starch grains in the flour are thoroughly cooked. Add the corn puree, salt and pepper and serve.

Whole-Berry Cranberry Sauce (87)

- 2 cups sugar
- 2 cups water
- 1 lb fresh cranberries

Boil sugar and water together 5 minutes. Add cranberries and boil without stirring until the skins pop open, about 5 minutes. Remove from heat and allow sauce to remain in pan until cool. Makes 1 quart.

Use 2 cups, and dry 2 cups to be used later. Pour 2 cups of sauce on a teflex sheet and dry. To reconstitute, place broken pieces of leather in bowl. Add 2 cups water and let stand 10 minutes. Stir with a fork several times (don't crush berries) to ensure proper reconstitution. Chill and serve.

Add less water and puree in blender for jellied cranberry sauce.

Cranberry-Orange Relish (88)

4 cups cranberries
1½ cups sugar
2 oranges (quartered & seeded)

Grind cranberries and oranges in food chopper, add sugar, and mix well. Chill some in the refrigerator for immediate use. Place two cups on teflex sheet and dry. To reconstitute, place two cups of boiling water over broken pieces of leather. Let stand 10 minutes and then stir well and place in refrigerator overnight. Stir again before serving.

Croutons (89)

24 slices leftover bread, with crusts trimmed
3 Tbsp Safflower oil
3 Tbsp butter

Cut bread into small cubes. Dry cubes in dehydrator. Saute in the oil and butter, stirring frequently, until golden brown on all sides. Makes 6 cups. Serve with soups and salads.

To make Garlic Croutons, just add 1 clove finely minced garlic to the oil and butter and saute until brown.

One pound of dry bread crumbs is equal to 5 cups.

Pumpernickel Croutons (90)

Cut 2 slices pumpernickel bread into ½-inch cubes. Dry in dehydrator until crisp. Toss with 1 tablespoon melted butter. Makes 1 cup.

Cookie Crusts (91)

1 cup butter or margarine
¼ cup sugar
2 cups flour
½ cup finely-chopped nuts

Combine butter and sugar. Add flour, mixing until dough forms. Add nuts. Press dough into the bottom and sides of two 9-inch pie pans. Bake at 375° F. about 15 minutes. Cool. This crust may be frozen for use at a later time.

Cornflake Crust (92)

4 Tbsp margarine
¼ cup sugar
2 tsp corn syrup
3 cups crushed cornflakes

Cream margarine, sugar, and corn syrup. Add crushed cornflakes. Press into a 9-inch pie pan. Bake in 375° F. oven about 10 minutes. Cool before filling.

Easy No-Roll Pastry Crust (93)

- 1½ cups flour
- 1½ tsp sugar
- ¾ tsp salt
- ½ cup salad oil
- 2 Tbsp milk

Combine flour, sugar and salt in 9-inch pie pan. Mix with fork. Beat oil and milk together with fork; mix into flour mixture until moistened. Press with fingers in even layer over bottom and up sides extending above rim. Flute edges. This is a rich crumbly crust.

Date Cake (94)

- 1½ cups dates, cut fine
- ½ tsp soda, dissolved in 1 cup boiling water
- ½ cup butter
- 1 cup sugar
- 1 tsp vanilla
- 1½ cups sifted cake flour
- 1 tsp baking powder
- ½ tsp cinnamon
- ¼ tsp salt

Pour soda and boiling water over dates. Cream butter, beat in sugar, add beaten eggs and vanilla. Add sifted dry ingredients alternately with water and dates. Bake in an 8 × 8-inch square greased pan at 350° F. for 40 minutes.

Date Cookies (95)

- ½ cup butter
- ½ cup granulated sugar
- ½ cup brown sugar
- 1 egg
- ½ tsp vanilla
- 2 cups flour
- ½ tsp cream tartar put into flour
- ½ tsp of soda dissolved in ½ Tbsp hot water
- 2 cups chopped dates
- ½ cup chopped pecans

Mix and make into two rolls. Place in the refrigerator over night; then slice about ½-inch thick and bake in 350° F. oven until top has dull crust, about 25 minutes.

Date Fig Fudge (96)

- 1 cup dates pitted
- 8 figs softened by steaming
- ½ cup coconut (see recipe #78)
- ½ cup pecans

Grind dates and figs in food grinder with medium blade. Add coconut and nuts and mix well. Press into 8 × 8-inch square pan that has been buttered. Refrigerate for several hours, cut and serve.

Date Sugar (General Instructions) (97)

If you are fortunate enough to be in an area where you can purchase fresh dates, then it's possible to dry them in the dehydrator.

To make date sugar from store-bought dates, pit the dates and place them in the blender with just a small amount of water. Use only 2 or 3 dates to start and add enough water to blend. Add dates a few at a time until you have the desired amount. It is then like date leather and is dried the same as leather. When it is very dry, return it to the blender and make a fine powder.

It is probably as expensive to make your own date sugar as it is to purchase it, but it is a higher quality when done at home. It is important not to dry over 130° F. or the dates taste scorched.

Date sugar can be used to sweeten yogurt, desserts prepared with whipping cream, granola, etc.

Dill Butter (98)

¼ cup butter
¼ tsp dill weed
½ tsp white wine vinegar

Combine ingredients and cream together until smooth. Spread on broiled fish.

Cross-Country Energy Bars (99)

2 cups natural cereal
½ cup wheat germ
2 Tbsp softened margarine
2 Tbsp honey
2 cups raisins

In a bowl, blend the cereal and wheat germ. With a fork work in margarine, then stir in honey. Pat ⅔ of crumb mixture into greased 8-inch square cake pan. Chop raisins as follows: Spray inside of blender container with natural vegetable spray. Whirl raisins, ½ cup at a time, on high speed, 8 to 10 seconds. Press chopped raisins on crumb layer. Sprinkle remaining crumbs on raisins. Pat firmly. Bake at 325° F. for 20 to 25 minutes. Cool 30 minutes before cutting. Makes 20. Wrap individually for convenience.

Candied Figs (General Instructions) (100)

There are many recipes for making candied figs. If figs are going to be dried whole they must have the natural wax protective coating treated to allow moisture to be removed. They should be steamed or treated in the microwave oven for 1 minute before drying whole. Candied figs do not need pretreatment.

For a *light* candied treatment, dip figs in:

1 cup light corn syrup
1 cup sugar
3 cups water

Heat to 212° F., add whole figs and simmer 10 minutes. Remove from heat and let stand in syrup 10 minutes longer; then lift out, drain, and dry. They will continue to drip so it would be wise to use a teflex sheet or a solid tray to prevent juices from getting on other foods in the dehydrator.

For a *heavy* candied fig treatment soak 30 figs for 10 minutes in a soda bath of

2 quarts water
2 Tbsp soda

Rinse well. Drop figs into a boiling syrup of

1½ cups sugar
2 cups water

Simmer for 20 minutes, remove from heat, cool. Cover and keep at room temperature for 24 hours. Repeat this process 3 more days. Drain figs, place on teflex sheet and place in dehydrator to dry.

Fig Chewies (101)

1 cup dehydrated fig slices
½ cup water
½ cup margarine
1 cup brown sugar, packed
1 egg, unbeaten
1 tsp vanilla
1¾ cups sifted flour
2 tsp baking powder
½ tsp salt
1½ cups grated coconut

Combine fig slices and water in a pan. Cook until reconstituted, about 5 minutes; cool. Cream margarine and brown sugar. Add unbeaten egg and vanilla; beat well. Add flour, baking powder, salt and figs. Mix thoroughly and drop dough by rounded teaspoonsful into grated coconut; roll to coat and form into balls. Bake on greased baking sheets at 375° F. for 12 to 15 minutes. Makes about 4 dozen cookies. Add a pecan or walnut half to the top of each cookie before baking if desired.

Fig Newtons (102)

- 1 cup sugar
- 1 cup shortening
- 1 cup honey
- 2 eggs, beaten
- Juice and rind of ½ lemon
- 6½ cups flour
- 2 tsp baking powder
- 1 tsp baking soda
- 1 tsp salt

Cream sugar, shortening and honey. Add beaten eggs, lemon juice and rind. Sift flour, baking powder, baking soda and salt 3 times, and add to creamed mixture. Roll quite thin; cut into strips about 6 inches long and 3 inches wide. Put filling* in center and lap sides over. Bake at 400° F. for 15 minutes. Cool and cut into desired size.

*Filling

- 4 cups ground dried figs
- 1 cup honey
- ½ cup water
- Juice of ½ lemon
- Juice of ½ orange

Combine ingredients and cook 20 minutes, stirring constantly to prevent sticking. Cool before putting into dough.

Fig Oatmeal Cookies (103)

- ½ cup shortening
- ½ cup butter
- 1½ cups dark brown sugar
- 2 eggs
- 1 tsp vanilla
- 2 cups sifted flour
- 1 tsp baking powder
- 1 tsp salt
- ½ tsp soda
- 2½ cups quick rolled oats
- Fig Filling*

Cream shortening, butter and sugar until fluffy. Add eggs and vanilla; beat well. Sift together flour, baking powder, salt and soda; add to creamed mixture and beat well. Stir in oats. Chill 1 hour. Roll half the dough at a time on well-floured pastry cloth to a little less than ¼ inch thickness. Cut with round cutter. Place 1 tablespoon Fig Filling on a half and cover with second half. Flute edges and pierce center top. Bake on an ungreased cookie sheet at 350° F. for 12 minutes. Makes about 30 cookies.

*Fig Filling

- 10 dried figs, chopped
- ½ cup water
- 3 Tbsp lemon juice
- ⅓ cup sugar
- 1 tsp grated lemon peel

Combine all ingredients; simmer 10 to 15 minutes.

Crunchy Fruit Stuffing (104)

- ½ cup chopped celery
- 1 Tbsp dehydrated onion
- ¼ cup butter
- 1½ qts crumbled cornbread
- 1½ qts dried bread crumbs
- 2 cups steamed chopped dried apricots*
- ¼ tsp poultry seasoning
- ¾ tsp salt
- ¼ tsp pepper
- 2½ to 2¾ cups hot broth

Saute the celery and onion in melted butter until tender. In a large bowl, combine the cornbread, bread crumbs, apricots and seasonings. Lightly stir in the hot broth; do not overmix. The exact amount of broth will depend on the dryness of the bread, but only enough to moisten dry ingredients will be needed. Spoon the stuffing loosely into the cavity of the turkey, leaving room for expansion during baking. Makes enough stuffing for a 12-pound turkey. It may also be baked in the oven at 350° F. for 30 minutes.

*Other fruits may be used in place of apricots.

Curried Fruit (Microwave) (105)

Place the following dried fruits in an 8 × 12-inch microwave dish:

- ½ cup apricot slices
- ½ cup pineapple tidbits
- ½ cup pear slices
- ½ cup peach slices
- ½ cup raisins
- ⅓ cup margarine
- ½ tsp curry powder
- ¾ cup brown sugar
- 15 maraschino cherries, halved
- ¾ cup slivered almonds

Cover with 2 cups of boiling water and let reconstitute until most of the moisture is absorbed. Melt margarine in a 2-cup measure. Stir in the curry and brown sugar. Microwave 1 minute. Pour over the reconstituted fruit. Microwave 12 minutes, basting and turning the dish each 4 minutes. Add halved cherries and nuts just before serving. Serve warm.

Dried Fruit Bars (106)

One cup well-packed pieces of dried fruits (not dates, raisins or coconut) rehydrated in ¾ cup boiling water.

- ½ tsp baking soda
- ½ cup oil
- 1 egg
- 1 cup oatmeal
- 1 cup flour
- ½ cup granulated sugar
- ½ cup brown sugar
- ½ tsp cinnamon
- ½ tsp salt
- ½ tsp nutmeg
- ½ tsp cloves

Add baking soda to the fruit mixture. Combine all ingredients and mix well. Spread evenly into a well-greased 9 × 13-inch baking pan. Bake at 350° F. for 20 minutes. Cool for 15 minutes before cutting into bars.

Dried Fruit Cookies (107)

- ½ cup margarine
- 10 oz miniature marshmallows
- 1 cup chopped apples
- 1 cup chopped raisins
- 2 cups graham cracker crumbs
- 1 cup chopped nuts
- 1 cup chopped prunes
- 1 tsp vanilla

Melt margarine and marshmallows together. Combine with other ingredients and mix well. Form into ½-inch balls and place on a teflex sheet on tray to dry for about 15 minutes or until crisp on the outside.

Dried Fruit Loaf (108)

- 1 cup brown sugar, packed
- 1 cup water
- 1 cup dried fruit, steamed and cut up
- ½ cup chopped nuts
- 1 Tbsp margarine
- ½ tsp salt
- 1 tsp soda
- 1 egg, beaten
- 2 cups flour

In a pan, mix together sugar, water, fruit, nuts, butter and salt; stir over medium heat until butter melts. Set aside. When cooled, stir in soda, then beaten egg, then flour. Bake in a greased 9 x 5 x 3-inch loaf pan at 350° F. for 1 hour. Cool. This loaf can be made from any dried fruit (such as apricots, prunes, or apples) or a combination of dried fruits. It makes a lovely gift when it is decorated.

Dried Fruit-Nut Balls (109)

- 1 cup pitted prunes
- 1 cup pitted dates
- 1 cup raisins
- 1 cup pitted cherries
- ½ cup wheat germ
- ½ tsp salt
- 2 Tbsp honey
- 2 Tbsp orange juice
- 1 tsp grated orange peel
- 1 cup shredded coconut
- 1 cup finely chopped pecans

Put prunes, dates, raisins, and cherries through a food chopper, using a fine blade. Knead in wheat germ, salt, honey, orange juice, orange peel, and shredded coconut. Form the mixture into 1-inch balls and roll in finely-chopped nuts. Keep in a tightly-covered container in the refrigerator. Makes 4 dozen.

The amount of moisture in dried fruit varies. If the mixture is too sticky, knead in a little more wheat germ; or if it is too dry, add a small amount of orange juice.

Fruit Butter (110)

- 2 lbs dehydrated fruit (apricots, peaches, pears, apples, etc.)
- 6 cups water
- 2 cups sugar

Combine the dried fruit and water in a large pan. Bring to a boil. Cover, and simmer 30 minutes. Stir in sugar thoroughly. Cover and simmer 30 minutes longer, stirring occasionally. The fruit should be cooked and stirred until it is soft and broken. Place in a blender and puree the fruit and juices. Let the fruit cool before blending to avoid steam burns. Store in covered jars in the refrigerator. Use the "butter" as a filling for cookies and muffins, or spread it on toast. Makes 1 quart.

No-Cook Fruit Butters (111)

(111A) Apple Butter—Use a 2-cup apple roll. Break the roll into pieces in the blender. Add ⅓ cup of apple juice and blend until smooth. Add ⅓ cup of brown sugar, ½ teaspoon of cinnamon, ¼ teaspoon allspice, ¼ teaspoon nutmeg, ¼ teaspoon cloves, a dash of salt, and 1 teaspoon lemon juice. Puree until the ingredients are thoroughly mixed. Chill and serve. Makes ¾ cup.

(111B) Peach Butter—Use a 2-cup peach roll. Break the roll into pieces in the blender. Add ⅓ cup of hot water and blend until smooth. Add ⅓ cup of sugar, 1 teaspoon cinnamon, and 1 teaspoon lemon juice. Puree until the ingredients are thoroughly mixed. Chill and serve. Makes ¾ cup.

(111C) Pear Butter—Use a 2-cup pear roll. Break the roll into pieces in the blender. Add ⅓ cup of hot water and blend until smooth. Add ¼ cup of sugar, 1 teaspoon of cinnamon, and 1 teaspoon lemon juice. Puree until the ingredients are thoroughly mixed. Chill and serve. Makes ¾ cup. Vary the recipe by using ⅓ cup of pineapple juice and omitting lemon juice.

(111D) Apricot Butter—Use a 2-cup apricot roll. Break the roll into pieces in the blender. Add ⅓ cup of hot water and blend until smooth. Add ⅓ cup of sugar, ½ teaspoon cinnamon, ½ teaspoon nutmeg and 1 teaspoon lemon juice. Puree until the ingredients are thoroughly mixed. Chill and serve. Makes ¾ cup. This is excellent when apricot nectar is used in place of the hot water.

(111E) Strawberry-Rhubarb Butter—Use a 2-cup strawberry-rhubarb roll. Break the roll into pieces in the blender. Add ⅓ cup of hot water and blend until smooth. Add ⅓ cup of sugar, and 1 teaspoon of lemon juice; puree until the ingredients are thoroughly mixed. Chill and serve. Makes ¾ cup.

(111F) Prune-Plum Butter—Use a 2-cup plum roll. Break the roll into pieces in the blender. Add ⅓ cup of hot water and blend until smooth. (Prune juice may be substituted for the hot water.) Add ⅓ cup sugar, ¼ teaspoon allspice, ¼ teaspoon ginger, ¼ teaspoon nutmeg, ¼ teaspoon cinnamon, 1 teaspoon grated orange peel. Puree until thoroughly blended. Chill and serve. Makes ¾ cup.

(111G) Apricot-Pineapple Butter—Use a 3-cup apricot roll. Break the roll into pieces in the blender. Add 1 cup crushed pineapple and juice, ½ teaspoon cinnamon, ⅓ cup of orange juice, 1 tablespoon lemon juice and ½ cup honey. Puree until ingredients are thoroughly mixed. Chill and serve.

Use butter in place of jam on toast or muffins. It is also good served on waffles, pancakes, or crepes.

Fruit Cake (112)

- 1 cup apricots
- 1 cup pears
- 1 cup raisins
- 1 cup dates
- 5 eggs
- ¼ cup water
- 1 tsp vanilla
- 1 cup pecans
- 1 cup walnuts
- 1 cup brazil nuts
- 2 cups flour
- 2 tsp baking powder
- ½ cup instant orange breakfast powder
- 1½ cups sugar
- ¾ tsp salt

Combine and mix the dry ingredients. Steam the apricots and pears for 3 minutes to soften them. Dredge the raisins in ¼ cup of the flour from the recipe. Lightly beat eggs, add water, vanilla, fruit, nuts and dry ingredients. Mix thoroughly. Bake in greased loaf pans at 325° F. until done, approximately 1 hour. Makes 4 loaves. Decorated, these make lovely Christmas gifts.

Apricot Glaze (Microwave) (112A)

- ½ cup dried apricots
- ¾ cup boiling water
- ½ cup white corn syrup

Place fruit and water in a glass dish in the microwave. Cook on high for 3 minutes. Reduce the setting to simmer and continue cooking for 5 minutes. Cool slightly and puree in blender until smooth. Press through a fine sieve and measure ¼ cup puree, add corn syrup, then place in microwave and boil rapidly for 3 minutes or until mixture is clear. Brush on cake while hot and apply decorations. A second coat may be brushed over decorations after they have dried to make a pretty all-over glaze. It may be necessary to reheat the glaze before using it the second time.

Hints for Fruit Cake Baking (112B)

Almost any container, if properly prepared, may be used to bake fruit cakes. Fill the chosen container with water to within one-half inch of the top edge. Then measure water to determine how much batter will be used. For larger loaf cakes, line pans with brown paper and grease with shortening. When using smaller pans such as small loaves, fancy molds, or juice cans, grease well. Cupcake pans may be lined with paper baking cups, or may be well greased. Some experienced cooks find foil a suitable liner for pans.

Fill larger pans ¾ full; smaller pans ⅓ full, or use a measured amount of batter as given in the recipe. Fill the pans with batter to within ½-inch of top edge. Cool the cakes thoroughly before wrapping. Wrap the cakes carefully in heavy foil, Saran or plastic bags. Store them in a cool, dry place. Age most fruit cakes 1 month or longer to mellow the flavors. Decorate or frost the cakes after aging them.

Pan Sizes and Baking Times

Pan Size	*Amount of Batter*	*Baking Time*
9 × 5 × 3-inch loaf pan	6½ cups	2½ hours
8½ × 4½ × 2½-inch loaf pan	5 cups	2 hours
5½ × 3 × 2½-inch loaf pan	1¾ cups	1½ hours
4½ × 1½-inch round foil pan	1 to 1¼ cups	1 hour 25 minutes
1 pound coffee can	3½ cups	1 hour 50 minutes
9 or 10-inch tube pan or mold	2½ quarts	3 to 3½ hours
8-inch ring mold	3 cups	1 hour 40 minutes
6-ounce juice can	½ cup	50 minutes
1¾ × 1-inch cupcake pans	1 rounded Tbsp	20 minutes
3 × 1½-inch cupcake pans	⅓ cup	40 minutes

Bake fruit cakes at 300° F. until the cake tests done in center. Place a shallow pan of hot water on the bottom of the oven to give a less heavy crust.

Fruit Frosty (113)

One cup dehydrated fruit rehydrated in ½ cup of water. Combine in a blender with 1 cup cracked ice and 1 cup unflavored yogurt, ¾ cup milk, and 3 tablespoons sugar; whirl until smooth. Blend the fruit and water for 2 minutes before adding the other ingredients. Use peaches, papaya, banana, strawberries, pineapple, etc.

Fruit Preserves (General Instructions) (114)

Because of the natural sugar content in dehydrated fruit, making preserves with dehydrated fruit reduces the amount of sugar required. It also reduces the cooking time required since the moisture has been removed by dehydration, and it is only necessary to put back enough moisture to reconstitute the fruit.

To make jam or butter, use fruit rolls. Fruit rolls have already been pureed so they are ideal to reconstitute and make jam or butter. Add just enough water to reconstitute, add sugar to taste, and cook to 9° F. higher than the temperature of boiling water. At sea level the temperature would be 221° F. Place in a sterilized container and cool. It is ready to serve. If a candy thermometer is not available, test the fruit by ready to serve. If a candy thermometer is not available, test the fruit by removing ½ teaspoonful of the cooked fruit, placing it on a sauce dish, and putting it into the deep freeze until cool to check the jell. If it is not thick enough, then it should be cooked a longer time.

To make preserves or conserves, use sliced fruits and reconstitute them by simmering in water until tender. Add sugar and cook to 9° F. above the temperature at which water boils. Spoon the preserves into a sterilized jar and cool.

Pineapple-Peach Preserves (Microwave) **(115)**

1 cup pear slices
¼ cup pineapple tidbits
¾ cup water
½ cup sugar

Place the pears and pineapple in a glass casserole with the water and cook on simmer, covered until tender. This will take about 10 minutes. Measure fruit. Add ½ cup sugar per cup of rehydrated, tender fruit. Continue to cook on simmer until the fruit is translucent and has reached the proper temperature. Stir after 2 minutes and check the temperature at 5 minutes. If the syrup is not thick enough, spoon the fruit pieces into sterilized jars and cook the syrup on simmer, uncovered to the desired thickness.

Preserves can be made on the surface unit following the same steps, except it will take a little longer for the fruit to cook.

Try some favorite preserve recipes made with dehydrated fruit. The aroma is supurb and the preserves are scrumptious.

Fruit Sauces (Microwave) **(116)**

Many fruit sauces can be made following these easy directions. It may be desirable to alter the amount of sugar.

⅓ cup sugar
1 Tbsp cornstarch
⅛ tsp salt
½ cup water

Mix the dry ingredients and place in a 4-cup glass measure. Stir in the water.

1 cup fruit slices reconstituted by steaming.
2 Tbsp lemon juice
1 Tbsp butter

Blend the fruit and lemon juice into the sugar mixture. Add butter. Microwave on high, uncovered for 3 to 4 minutes, or until mixture boils. Stir each minute until smooth.

Serve with sponge, angel or pound cake.

Fruit Soup (Microwave) **(117)**

1 cup dehydrated pears
1 cup dehydrated apricots
1 cup dehydrated peaches
½ cup raisins
½ lemon, thinly sliced
2 quarts water

Combine the above ingredients in a 3-quart glass casserole. Stir in the following ingredients:

1 cup sugar
2 Tbsp minute tapioca
½ tsp salt
2 sticks cinnamon

Microwave on high, covered, just until it comes to a boil—about 15 minutes. Microwave on medium, covered, 20 minutes, or until the fruits are tender. May be served hot or cold. Remove cinnamon sticks before serving.

Fruit Syrup (Waffles and Pancakes) **(118)**

Sprinkle 1 tablespoon of gelatin in ¼ cup cold water. Let stand until thickened. Add ⅓ cup boiling water. Stir until dissolved.

Place a 2-cup fruit leather roll into a blender. Add two cups of boiling water and puree until smooth. Add 1 cup sugar and the gelatin mixture and blend until thoroughly mixed. Reheat for hot syrup, or place in refrigerator to cool.

Choose any fruit. This makes a fluffy syrup that is not overly sweet.

Frozen Fruit Yogurts **(119)**

Basic Frozen Yogurt

3 eggs, separated
¼ tsp salt
¼ tsp cream of tartar
4 Tbsp sugar
2 qts plain yogurt

Lightly beat the egg yolks; stir in about ½ cup of the hot fruit mixture and then stir the yolk mixture back into the fruit. Cool to room temperature.

Combine egg whites, salt and cream of tartar; beat until soft peaks form. Add sugar gradually and continue beating until stiff peaks form.

Place yogurt into a large bowl; smooth out any lumps and fold the fruit mixture (choice of fruit mixture from below) into yogurt until well blended. Gently fold the egg whites into the yogurt-fruit mixture. Pour mixture into freezer container and freeze. Assemble freezer and follow manufacturer's directions, using 4 parts ice to 1 part rock salt.

Apricot-Orange Mixture

- 4 cups dehydrated apricots plus 4 cups water
- 1⅓ cups sugar
- 1 Tbsp lemon juice
- ½ cup orange juice
- 1 Tbsp vanilla

Berry Mixture

- 4 cups dehydrated berries plus 4 cups water
- 1⅓ cups sugar
- 1 Tbsp lemon juice
- 1 Tbsp vanilla

Nectarine Mixture

- 4 cups dehydrated nectarines plus 4 cups water
- 1⅓ cups firmly packed brown sugar
- 2 Tbsp lemon juice

Peach Mixture

- 4 cups dehydrated peaches plus 4 cups water
- 1⅓ cups firmly packed brown sugar
- 2 Tbsp lemon juice
- 1 Tbsp vanilla
- 1 tsp cinnamon

Place the water, sugar and fruit into a 3-quart pan. Bring to a boil, reduce heat to medium and cook, stirring constantly, until fruit softens and partially disintegrates. Break up any large pieces with a fork. Remove from heat and stir in the fruit juices, spice and flavorings suggested for the fruit being used.

Gooseberry Dumplings (120)

- 4 cups gooseberries reconstituted in 2 cups boiling water, simmer for 5 minutes, drain and reserve syrup
- ¾ cup sugar
- 2 Tbsp cornstarch
- Dumpling Batter*
- Whipped Topping (see recipe #286)

Combine the gooseberry syrup, sugar and cornstarch in a deep skillet. Cook until thickened and clear. Stir in gooseberries. Drop dumpling batter by tablespoonfuls on top of the fruit, making 6 dumplings. Cover and cook gently for 20 minutes. Serve warm with whipped topping.

***Dumpling Batter**

1 cup flour
2 Tbsp sugar
1 tsp baking powder
¼ tsp salt
1 Tbsp melted margarine
½ cup milk

Sift the dry ingredients together. Add the margarine and milk. Stir just to moisten. Drop by tablespoonfuls onto the hot gooseberries. Cook as directed.

Graham Crackers (121)

3½ cups graham flour or whole wheat flour
½ tsp salt
½ tsp baking powder
¾ cup packed brown sugar
¾ cup butter
¾ cup water

Combine the flour, salt and baking powder. Beat the sugar and butter until creamy. Add the flour mixture and water, alternately, mixing well after each addition. Cover the dough and let it stand at room temperature 30 minutes.

Divide the dough into 2 equal portions. Pat each portion on a greased cookie sheet into a ½-inch thick rectangle. Roll the dough evenly to 12 × 15 inches. Cut it into 3-inch squares. Bake at 325° F. for 30 minutes or until lightly browned. Cool on a wire rack. Makes 40.

Graham Cracker Crust (122)

1¼ cups graham cracker crumbs
⅓ cup butter or margarine
3 Tbsp powdered sugar

Combine the crumbs and sugar in a medium-sized bowl. Stir in the melted butter or margarine until thoroughly blended. Pack the mixture firmly into a 9-inch pan and press it firmly to the bottom and sides, bringing the crumbs evenly up to the rim. Chill 1 hour before filling, or bake in 350° F. oven 8 minutes. Cool, chill and fill.

Graham Cracker Crust (Microwave) (123)

⅔ cup butter
2½ cups graham cracker crumbs
½ cup granulated sugar

In a bowl, melt the butter at high for 1 to 1½ minutes. Add crumbs and the ½ cup sugar. Mix well. Press into two 9-inch pie plates. Bake uncovered at medium high for 2 minutes; press out bubbles. Cool.

Basic Granola (124)

- 4 cups oatmeal
- ½ cup sesame seed
- ½ tsp vanilla
- ½ cup wheat germ
- ¾ tsp salt
- ½ cup honey
- ⅓ cup vegetable oil

Mix all ingredients thoroughly. Let stand 1 hour so the oats will absorb flavor. Place on dehydrator trays and dry from 1 to 3 hours according to personal taste for crispness. This makes about 2 trays.

Spiced Granola (125)

To the above recipe #124, add the following:

- 1 cup dehydrated shredded coconut
- ½ cup sunflower seeds
- 1½ tsp cinnamon
- 1 tsp nutmeg
- 1 cup raisins

Apple-Cinnamon Granola (126)

To the above recipe #125, add the following:

- 1 cup finely chopped pecans
- 1 cup cut-up dehydrated apple slices

Peanut Butter Granola (127)

Omit oil from the Basic Granola recipe and add 1 cup creamy or chunky peanut butter.

Quick Breakfast Snack (Granola) (128)

To the Apple-Cinnamon Granola recipe, add ½ cup date crystals.

Granola is most often served as a breakfast food. It can also be used as a snack or an ingredient in desserts, cookies, or main dishes. Just add the fruit—apricots, apples, peaches, bananas, etc., nuts or coconut and have a variety.

Granola (Microwave) (129)

- 3 cups uncooked quick or old-fashioned oats
- 1 cup shredded dehydrated coconut
- 1 cup pecan pieces
- ¼ cup melted margarine
- 1½ tsp cinnamon
- ½ tsp salt
- ¼ cup honey
- ⅔ cup raisins

Combine all ingredients except raisins in large bowl; mix well. Sprinkle into an 11 × 8-inch glass baking dish. Cook on high 8 to 10 minutes or until golden brown, stirring after every 2 minutes of cooking. Stir in raisins. Sprinkle onto cookie sheet to cool. Store in tightly-covered container. Makes 6 cups.

Granola Brownies (130)

- ½ cup margarine
- 2 squares unsweetened chocolate
- 1 cup sugar
- 2 eggs
- 1 tsp vanilla
- ½ cup Spiced Granola (see recipe #125)
- ½ cup flour
- ½ tsp baking powder
- ¼ tsp salt
- ½ cup chopped nuts

Melt margarine and chocolate in a large saucepan. Remove from heat. Blend in the sugar and eggs and beat well. Stir in the remaining ingredients. Spread into a greased 8-inch square pan. Bake at 350° F. for 25 to 30 minutes. Cut into bars while still warm.

Granola-Cream Cheese Crunch (131)

- 2 cups Apple-Cinnamon Granola (see recipe #126)
- ¼ cup butter, melted
- 1 cup cream cheese, softened
- 1⅓ cups sweetened condensed milk
- ⅓ cup lemon juice
- 1 tsp vanilla
- Sliced strawberries

Mix granola and butter thoroughly. Reserve ⅔ cup of the granola mixture. Press the remaining mixture into an ungreased square pan, 9 × 9 × 2-inches. Beat the cream cheese in a small mixer bowl until light and fluffy. Stir in milk gradually. Add lemon juice and vanilla and stir until well blended. Pour over granola mixture. Sprinkle remaining granola mixture over top. Refrigerate 3 to 4 hours, or until firm. Top with fresh-sliced strawberries.

Granola Fudge Sundae Squares (132)

- 1 pt vanilla ice cream, brick style
- ¾ cup Spiced Granola (see recipe #125)
- 3 squares unsweetened chocolate
- 3 Tbsp margarine
- ¾ cup sugar
- ½ cup half-and-half
- 1 tsp vanilla
- Maraschino cherries

Press about ½ cup granola onto all sides of a thoroughly-frozen pint of ice cream. Place the coated ice cream on a pre-chilled cookie sheet. Freeze several hours until firm.

Melt the chocolate and margarine together in the top of a double boiler over hot, not boiling, water. Stir in sugar. Cook over hot water 5 minutes longer, stirring frequently. Stir in half-and-half and vanilla. Cook over hot water until blended.

To serve, cut ice cream into 6 pieces. Pour warm fudge sauce over each slice, sprinkle with remaining granola and top with maraschino cherries. Serves 6. Extra fudge sauce may be refrigerated for use at a later time.

Granola Hearth Bread (133)

- 3 to 3½ cups flour
- 1 cup Basic Granola (see recipe #124)
- 2 tsp salt
- 2 pkgs active dry yeast
- ¼ cup molasses
- 1¼ cups water
- ¼ cup oil
- 1 egg

In a large mixer bowl, combine 1½ cups flour, granola, salt and dry yeast. Heat the water and oil until warm. Add warm liquid, molasses and egg to flour mixture. Blend at lowest speed until moistened. Beat 3 minutes at medium speed. By hand, stir in another 1½ to 2 cups flour to form a stiff batter. Cover dough and allow to raise in a dehydrator until doubled. Stir down dough. Spoon into a generously greased 2-quart casserole. Bake at 350° F. for 45 to 50 minutes, or until the loaf sounds hollow when lightly tapped. Remove from oven, cool, brush with margarine, and sprinkle with coarse salt, if desired.

Crunchy Granola Pilaf (134)

- 2 Tbsp margarine
- 2 Tbsp finely chopped onion
- 1 cup chicken broth
- ½ cup bulgur wheat
- ¼ cup dehydrated mushrooms, chopped
- ¼ tsp dried oregano
- ¼ tsp salt
- 1½ cups basic granola

Heat the margarine in a fry pan over medium heat until melted. Add onion and cook until tender. Stir in broth, bulgur, mushrooms, oregano and salt. Cover and heat to boiling; reduce heat. Simmer 15 minutes. Stir in granola and serve. Serves 4.

Granny Smith Granola (135)

- 3 Granny Smith apples
- 2 cups uncooked oatmeal
- 2 Tbsp brown sugar
- 1 tsp salt
- ½ cup slivered almonds
- ½ tsp cinnamon
- 1 Tbsp honey in
- ¼ cup water

Quarter, peel and core apples. Grate on the large side of the grater. Place in a bowl with the other ingredients and toss lightly until thoroughly mixed. Place the mixture on a solid tray or teflex-lined tray and dry for 2 to 3 hours. This is very crunchy. For a more tender granola, add ¼ cup vegetable oil.

Grape Leather Toaster Tarts (136)

- ½ cup margarine
- ¼ cup creamy peanut butter
- 1 cup firmly packed brown sugar
- 1 egg
- 3⅔ cups flour
- ⅛ tsp soda
- ¼ tsp salt
- ¼ cup hot water
- Grape Leather Jam (see recipe #137)

In the large bowl of a mixer, cream the margarine and peanut butter until smooth. Add sugar and egg. Mix flour, soda and salt and add alternately with water to the peanut butter mixture.

Divide the dough in half. Roll on a lightly-floured surface to a 15 × 9-inch rectangle. Cut into five 9 × 3-inch rectangles. Cut the rectangles in half crosswise. Spread 2 teaspoons of grape leather jam over one-half of each rectangle, leaving ½ inch around edges. Lift the uncovered portion over the covered portion. Press together with a fork and prick top. Roll out other half in the same way. Bake at 400° F. for 7 minutes or until browned around edges. Cool and wrap separately. Toast just before serving. Tarts may be frozen. Bake tarts for 10 minutes if they are not going to be toasted.

Any fruit leather would be good substituted in this recipe. Strawberry-rhubarb would be excellent.

Grape Leather Jam (137)

One 1-cup grape leather roll reconstituted by adding 2½ tablespoons boiling water and ⅓ cup sugar. Puree in blender until smooth.

Herbs (General Instructions) (138)

Use a light hand with herbs. When in doubt, a little is better than too much. Dried herbs and fresh herbs may be used interchangeably, but remember the dried herb is concentrated and will require only one-fourth to one-third as much as is called for fresh.

Crush the dried herbs between the palms of the hands. Crush the seeds with a mortar and pestle. This releases their essential oils and brings out the flavor.

For best flavor, slow-cooking dishes (stews, ragouts, soups) should have the herbs added during the last hour of cooking.

To prevent specks of herbs from being visible in cream sauces, tie the seasonings in several thicknesses of cheesecloth.

Seasonings with similar characteristics may be used interchangeably: Allspice and Cloves, Sweet Basil and Tarragon, Sesame and Poppy Seed. Don't be afraid to experiment.

Bouquet Garni (139)

Tie the following herbs in a cheesecloth bag for adding to soup or stock. Use coarsely-crumbled herbs.

- ½ tsp dried parsley
- ¼ tsp thyme
- ¼ tsp marjoram
- ½ bay leaf
- ½ tsp dried celery leaves

These seasonings can also be powdered and used to season beef, lamb, veal and poultry. Use ½ to 1 teaspoon for 4 pounds of meat. Rub in well. If using ground meat, mix along with other ingredients.

Fines Herbes (140)

Use ½ teaspoon for 4 servings. Crush herbs before adding. This is a balanced blend of sweet herbs. Use ½ teaspoon for 4 servings. Use with savory sauces, nonsweet egg dishes, such as omelets, and all cheese dishes. When used in omelets, mix with the eggs before cooking. Use equal parts of parsley, chives, basil, chervil and tarragon.

Hiker's Snack (141)

Some people call this "Gorp." To me that denotes something I would not want to eat. Hiker's Snack depicts a delicious combination of high-energy foods to nibble on for the energy to make it to the top of the hill. Everything goes into this mix.

- 1 cup sunflower seeds
- 1 cup carob chips
- 1 cup raisins
- 1 cup dehydrated apricots
- 1 cup dehydrated pears
- 1 cup dehydrated strawberries
- 1 cup broken cashews
- 1 cup sliced coconut
- 1 cup dehydrated apples
- 1 cup dehydrated peaches
- 1 cup slivered almonds
- 1 cup dehydrated nectarines

Mix well and store in a tightly covered container.

Caution: Omit carob chips when hiking during hot summer weather.

When you get too old to hike, then you settle back and call the mix

T.V. Snack (142)

You can add a few more calories, relax, enjoy it, and take off the extra pounds at the exercise gym.

- 1 cup sunflower seeds
- 1 cup brazil nuts
- 1 cup butterscotch morsels
- 1 cup raisins
- 1 cup pitted cherries
- 1 cup pineapple tidbits (dehydrated)
- 1 cup broken cashews
- 1 cup sliced coconut
- 1 cup whole almonds
- 1 cup cut dates
- 1 cup papaya chunks
- 1 cup pecans

Mix well. Seal some in a Seal-a-Meal bag and store in a deepfreeze for future use. This also makes a lovely gift package when placed in a compote and tied with a beautiful bow.

To make the sliced coconut, break open a fresh coconut, pare off the brown skin and shave with a potato peeler to make curls. Dry in a dehydrator for about 2 hours or until crunchy.

Hors d'oeuvres (143)

Crunchy raisin stalks make an appetizer tray. Blend peanut butter with a little orange marmalade. Add some Black Monukka raisins and stuff stalks of celery. Watch them disappear.

Ice Cream (144)

Use any dehydrated fruits or berries to make ice cream. Just add them to the milk as it goes into the refrigerator to stand undisturbed for 10 minutes. Steam the fruits to soften them, and cut them into small pieces so they will be evenly distributed throughout the ice cream.

Four-Quart Freezer

6	rennet tablets	2⅔	cups whipping cream
¼	cup cold water	1	Tbsp vanilla
1¾	qts milk (not canned)	1	tsp lemon
2⅔	cups sugar	1½	cups steamed fruit

Disperse rennet tablets in cold water. Combine milk, sugar, and cream and heat to lukewarm (110° F.). Remove from heat and add flavoring and steamed fruit. Add dissolved rennet tablets quickly and pour into freezing container. Let stand undisturbed for 10 minutes. Follow directions with hand or electric freezer and freeze.

Suggested Fruits: Strawberries, raspberries, blackberries, blueberries, boysenberries, apricots, peaches and nectarines. Leathers can also be used by rehydrating them in boiling water to a fine puree. Place 1½ cups leather pieces in blender and add boiling water to the 1½-cup measure. Puree until smooth. Add to the milk mixture before placing in the refrigerator. Pumpkin ice cream is delicious. Add some pumpkin pie spice while blending the leather. Taste to see how sweet it is. It may be necessary to add some honey or sugar to sweeten it slightly.

Jam Leather Tart (145)

Basic Pastry

1 cup butter
½ cup dairy sour cream
1½ cups flour (dipping method)

Cut butter into the flour with a pastry blender until completely mixed. Stir in sour cream until thoroughly blended. Divide dough into 2 parts; wrap each and refrigerate 8 hours. Heat oven to 350° F. Roll pastry on floured pastry cloth to 1/16th inch; cut into 2-inch shapes. Cut a small hole in the center of half of the shapes. Brush with sugar glaze* and place on top of the plain shapes. Fill the hole with ½ teaspoon jam.** Bake 20 to 25 minutes. Makes about 40.

Sugar Glaze

3 Tbsp sugar
1 Tbsp water

Mix well.

****Leather Jam***

1 cup seedless boysenberry leather
¼ cup boiling water
2 Tbsp sugar

Place in the blender and let stand for 5 minutes. Puree until smooth.

Foolproof Jelly Roll (146)

All you need are three drinking glasses (all the same size), the ingredients, and an accurate eye. The eggs, flour and sugar are each placed in the separate glasses at equal levels. With a little mixing and baking, the result is a perfect jelly roll. The sponge cake will be light and airy and easy to roll—just the way it is supposed to be.

3 drinking glasses (same size)
4 eggs
Sifted flour
Sugar
½ tsp salt
½ tsp cream of tartar
1 tsp vanilla or lemon extract
Powdered sugar
1 cup filling

Break eggs into the first drinking glass. Spoon the sifted flour into the second glass, to reach the same level as the eggs. Repeat for sugar, in the third glass. In a mixer bowl, beat eggs with salt, cream of tartar, and vanilla until thick. Add sugar gradually, beating at least 4 minutes. Add flour in three portions, folding quickly and thoroughly. Spread the batter in a waxed paper-lined 11 × 15-inch jelly roll pan. Bake at 375° F. for 15 minutes. Invert immediately onto a towel sprinkled with powdered sugar. Jelly rolls are neater to roll if you use the towel trick: when the roll is filled and ready, start the first tight turn with your hand, then lift the towel higher and higher, and the jelly roll will roll by itself.

See recipes for fruitbutters and jams to be used as filling for jelly roll.

Jerky (General Instructions) (147)

Use fresh, partially-frozen meat for jerky. Lean meat makes a more quality product. Jerky can be made from beef, deer, buffalo, smoked turkey, salmon, ham and, would you believe?, even shark. The University of California Extension Service has a recipe for shark jerky. All sharks can be made into jerky, but the Blue Shark is especially good prepared as jerky.

Jerky can be made with a liquid marinade or with dry seasonings which are applied without water. Jerky, marinated in water, absorbs water and takes a longer time to dry. Dry seasoning sprinkled over meat draws the moisture out of it in the curing process. It doesn't require as long a time to dry, but it does require refrigeration while curing.

The Tupperware Season-Serve* is the ideal container for marinating jerky, but any plastic, glass, or stainless steel pan with a tight-fitting

---

*Distributed by *Dart Industries, Inc.*

lid will do the job. Stir occasionally so that all pieces of meat receive equal flavoring. Drain, place on trays, and dry. When properly dried, the strips of meat should bend but not break.

Beef Jerky (147A)

To make beef jerky, purchase a 1-inch thick round steak that has very little marbled fat. Cut the meat with the grain to avoid shattering. Trim all visible fat and slice in ¼-inch strips. Partially frozen meat is easier to slice. This gives a jerky strip that is 1-inch by ¼-inch.

Marinade #1

1 Tbsp liquid smoke	4 lbs meat
¼ cup vinegar	1 tsp salt
1 pkg Adolph's meat marinade*	¾ cup water

Place the marinade in a container, and place the meat strips into the marinade. Place the lid on the container and shake the meat so that all pieces are exposed to the sauce. Shake the container several times during the marinating time so that all pieces of meat receive equal flavoring. Depending on individual taste, it should be marinated from 45 minutes to one hour. Drain, place on trays, and dry. After 6 hours, remove a piece of meat from the dehydrator, let it cool, and check to see if it is dry.

Marinade #2

¼ cup soy sauce	1 Tbsp salt
½ cup grape juice	½ tsp garlic salt
½ Tbsp lemon pepper	½ Tbsp liquid smoke
½ Tbsp Tobasco Sauce	2 cups boiling water

Combine all ingredients and pour over 4 pounds of round steak sliced for jerky. Marinate 45 minutes. Drain and place in the dehydrator at 145° F. Check after 4 hours.

Ham, Smoked Turkey and Smoked Chicken Jerky (148)

It is not necessary to marinate ham, smoked turkey or smoked chicken. It has already been seasoned. Just cut the strips the desired size and place in the dehydrator to dry. Test for dryness after 4 hours.

Smoked Salmon Jerky (149)

Use the same marinade for Salmon as for beef jerky. Cut the salmon in ¾-inch steaks and place in marinade. Remember that the larger the piece, the longer it takes to dry. It also takes longer to reconstitute.

---

*Distributed by *Adolph's, Ltd.*

Dry-Cured Jerky (150)

- ¼ cup soy sauce
- 1 Tbsp Worcestershire Sauce
- ½ tsp pepper
- ½ tsp garlic salt
- 1 tsp onion salt
- 1 tsp hickory smoke-flavored salt
- 4 lbs meat

Combine the soy sauce, Worcestershire, pepper, garlic, onion and smoke-flavored salt in a bowl. Stir until the seasonings are dissolved. Pat mixture thoroughly over surface of cut meat. Cover and let stand 4 to 6 hours depending on individual taste. Place in tightly covered container in the refrigerator. Stir occasionally for a more even penetration of flavors. Shake off any excess liquid, arrange strips of meat close together but not overlapping on dehydrator trays, and dry. Check after 4 hours to see if jerky is dry.

Gluten Jerky (151)

Gluten is the protein of wheat. After wheat grain is ground into flour, the gluten can be separated through a special process. Gluten may also be purchased commercially. Gluten may be flavored like jerky for vegetarians. This allows them to enjoy a protein snack food. There are good books available to teach the process of making gluten.

Gluten Jerky Marinade (Microwave)

- 3 cups raw gluten (Let stand 30 minutes before rolling)
- 1 pkg Adolph's Steak Sauce Flavor Marinade*
- 2 Tbsp beef base
- ⅓ cup vinegar
- 1 cup water
- 1 Tbsp liquid smoke
- 1 Tbsp Kitchen Bouquet**

Roll gluten into a 9 × 12-inch rectangle shape ¼-inch thick. Cut 3/8-inch strips 9 inches long. Place gluten strips in a microwave utility pan. Cover wth sauce. Cook, covered on high 5 minutes. Turn gluten strips over in pan to distribute sauce. Continue cooking on simmer for 25 to 35 minutes or until sauce has been absorbed into gluten. Turn gluten strips several times for better penetration of flavor. Arrange strips of gluten close together but not overlapping on dehydrator trays, and dry. Check after 3 hours for dryness test. It should be chewy not brittle, when cool.

For those people who do not have microwave ovens, follow the same procedure in preparation. Place the sauce in a frying pan and bring it

---

*Distributed by *Adolph's, Ltd.*

***Grocery Store Products Company*

to a boil. Drop gluten strips into boiling sauce, reduce heat and simmer, covered, until all sauce is absorbed. Turn gluten strips several times for better penetration of flavor. Arrange strips of gluten on trays, and dry. Check for dryness.

Note: Because gluten jerky is made from wheat, it hardens as it ages; therefore, do not plan to keep it more than one week.

Leathers (General Instructions) **(152)**

Fruit Leathers make good snack foods, baby foods, shakes, ice cream, sauces, syrups, yogurt flavorings, and puree for a variety of dessert recipes.

To prepare fresh fruit for leathers, wash the fruit, remove pits and peels that would be objectionable (fuzzy peaches, grainy pears). It is possible to use overripe fruit to make leathers, but do not use moldy or soured fruit. To make a pretty, natural-colored fruit roll, just dip the sliced fruit into a sodium bisulfite solution for 2 minutes, and then drain it before placing it in the blender to puree. When this is done, apricot is orange, pear is creamy white, apple is white and pineapple is pale yellow. It is only necessary to dip fruits that oxidize.

Juice pulps make good leather. After the fruit has been pressed through the colander to remove pits, skins and seeds, it can be combined with a fresh fruit to make interesting combinations. After making grape juice, use the pulp in combination with apples to make grape-apple leather. After making apple juice, combine the pulp with some fresh cranberries in the blender and puree to make cran-apple leather. Tomato pulp makes a good concentrate for paste or sauce when seasoned.

Puree 2 cups of fruit, sweeten if desired, add spices, nuts, coconut, etc., and pour onto plastic wrap, solid sheets, Teflex sheets, or plastic sheets to dry. The leather should be approximately one-fourth inch deep. Two cups of puree will cover most standard dehydrator trays to the correct depth. Once dehydrated, it is difficult to know how much fruit is contained in a roll; therefore, it is advisable to always use 2 cups of pureed fruit with each roll of leather made. When reconstituting, if a recipe calls for 1 cup of pureed fruit, break the fruit roll in half and break one half into pieces. Set the other half aside for future use. Place the broken pieces into a measuring cup and finish filling the cup to the top with liquid (water, broth, juice). To make applesauce, for example, puree the broken pieces of apple leather and apple juice until smooth and add sugar or honey and cinnamon. This makes 1 cup of applesauce.

It takes 9 to 12 hours for a fruit roll to dry. When the leather (except cherry) is soft but not tacky, test it by cooling a piece. It should lift off from the sheet and roll without breaking. If it breaks, it was dried too much. Cherry leather will remain sticky when it is dry.

When the leather is dry, remove it from the sheet and place it on a piece of plastic wrap. Roll the plastic wrap and the leather together into a roll. This prevents the leather from sticking to itself. Label each roll and place it into storage. If the leather is overdried, break it into small chips and serve it as a snack, or it can be rehydrated to make sauce, shakes, etc.

Plastic Wrap

Use plastic wrap cut to fit the tray when drying fruit rolls, dehydrating soups, or making cookies. Fold back a double thickness on the side edges of the tray for weight so it will not blow back into the fruit and prevent it from drying. (Taping the edge will prevent its blowing into the leather, but it will also cause the tray to become sticky and hard to clean.) After the roll is dry, remove the fruit and re-roll it on the opposite, clean side of the wrap. If the fruit is rolled on the side on which it was dried, it will stick to the tiny particles of food that remain on the wrap.

Solid Sheets

With solid accessory sheets you can dry almost any creamy or semi-liquid food such as soups, fruit purees, dressings, gravy, yogurt or casseroles. For easier removal of purees, etc., season the solid sheet with liquid lecithen or spray it with a non-stick vegetable cooking preparation. The puree is easier to remove from a seasoned solid sheet.

Teflex Sheets

Teflex is a new space-age product used in food preparation. It has a non-stick surface, is flexible and easy to clean. Teflex is coated with Dupont Teflon, six times thicker than the surface on modern cookware. It is durable and can be used repeatedly Because it is nonporous, it will hold liquid purees. To clean Teflex, simply wash it with warm soap and water and dry. It is excellent to use when making fruit rolls, dehydrating soups, granola, cookies or any small food that can fall through the mesh screen.

Plastic Sheets

Mylar or food-grade heavy plastic may be used to dry purees. Because of its weight, it will remain flat and will not blow into the liquid; however, it is sometimes hard to remove the leather. If this is a problem, it may be necessary to pretreat the sheets with a non-stick vegetable spray. The finished product is then easier to remove.

It is not advisable to use *plastic bread bags* (puree does not dry as fast), *wax paper* (puree permeates the paper and can not be separated), or *aluminum foil* (it must be greased or the puree will not release, and it does not dry as fast).

Apricot Leather (153)

Wash apricots thoroughly, remove pits, dip in sodium bisulfite solution for 2 minutes, drain, and puree. Pour onto a solid sheet and dry. Use overripe apricots for flavorful leather.

Chunky Pineapple Leather (154)

Place cleaned, fresh pineapple into a blender and chop it into small pieces. Do not puree. Pour onto sheets and dry. Measure the fruit and, when reconstituting, place broken pieces of leather into a cup and fill the cup with pineapple juice or water. Allow it to stand, stirring occasionally until soft and the consistency of crushed pineapple.

Strawberry-Rhubarb Leather (155)

Clean rhubarb and strawberries thoroughly. Use 1 cup of rhubarb, 2 cups of strawberries, and 2 tablespoons of honey or white Karo syrup. Rhubarb will be stringy unless it is cooked before it is pureed. Simmer 1 tablespoon of water and rhubarb for 2 or 3 minutes. Place all ingredients into the blender and puree.

Leather Cake (156)

- ½ cup shortening
- 1 cup sugar
- 3 eggs
- 1 cup leather reconstituted to consistency of jam
- 2 cups flour
- 1 tsp soda
- ¼ tsp salt
- ½ tsp cinnamon
- ½ tsp ground cloves
- ½ tsp nutmeg
- 1 cup buttermilk
- ½ cup nuts
- ½ cup raisins

Cream the shortening and sugar. Beat in eggs one at a time. Add leather puree.* Sift the dry ingredients together and add alternately with buttermilk. Stir in nuts and raisins. Pour into a greased and floured 9 × 13-inch loaf pan. Bake at 350° F. for 40 minutes or until done. Frost when cool.

*Break the leather into pieces, fill a cup with water, and puree in a blender to make a smooth sauce consistency. If the leather is very tart, it may be necessary to increase the sugar by ¼ cup.

Lemon-Cream Cheese Dessert (157)

3 cups Cheerios, finely crushed
1/3 cup margarine, melted
1 tsp cinnamon
1 cup cream cheese, softened
1 1/3 cups sweetened condensed milk
1/4 cup lemon juice
1 tsp vanilla

Heat oven to 350° F. Mix cereal, margarine and cinnamon in small bowl; reserve 2 tablespoons. Press remaining cereal mixture in ungreased baking pan, 8 x 8 x 2-inches. Bake 12 minutes; cool.

Beat cream cheese in large mixer bowl until light and fluffy. Mix in milk gradually. Stir in lemon juice and vanilla. Pour over baked cereal mixture in pan. Sprinkle reserved cereal mixture over top. Refrigerate until firm, 3-4 hours. Top with fruit sauce.* Serve.

***Fruit Sauce**

Pour 1 1/4 cups water over 2 1/2 cups dehydrated boysenberries in a 2-quart pan. Bring to a boil; add 1/3 cup sugar and thicken with 1 1/4 tablespoons cornstarch dissolved in 1/4 cup cold water. Cook, stirring continuously, until clear. Cool and serve over cheese dessert.

Other fruits may be used by varing spices and sugar content.

Lemon Sauce (158)

1/2 cup sugar
2 Tbsp cornstarch
1 cup water
1/4 cup soft margarine
1 Tbsp grated lemon rind
3 Tbsp lemon juice

Mix the sugar and cornstarch in a 2-quart saucepan. Stir water in gradually. Stir over medium heat until mixture boils. Boil and stir about 1 minute more or until the mixture is thick and clear. Remove from heat and stir in butter, rind and juice. Serve warm over puddings.

Diastatic Malt (General Instructions) (159)

Just what is diastatic malt? Diastase develops in grains when they sprout. Its function is to break down the starches in the grain to sugars. When diastatic malt is added to bread dough, it breaks down the starch in the wheat flour and releases the sugars that feed the yeast cells. Yeast cells can release sugar from starches, but they do it more slowly and that is why bread recipes call for sugar, honey, or molasses to help speed the process. By using diastatic malt, you can have high and fast-rising bread that is sweet. This is an advantage for hypoglycemics and diabetics.

To make diastatic malt one can use barley, wheat, or rye. Wheat and rye are more readily available than barley and a combination of wheat and rye makes a more sweet malt powder.

Soak ½ cup wheat and ½ cup rye in tepid water overnight. Then place in a sprouter and rinse with tepid water and drain twice daily, keeping the sprouts moist. When the sprout is about the length of the grain, place it on a teflex sheet in the dehydrator and dry at 145° F. until all of the moisture is gone. When the sprouts are dry, grind or blend in a blender to a powder. Use about 1 teaspoon of diastatic malt per two loaves of bread. If used in excess it will cause sticky, soggy bread. One cup of sprouts will yield enough diastatic malt to make 150 loaves of bread. After the sprouts are ground they will turn rancid if they are not stored in the refrigerator.

Meat (General Instructions) **(160)**

For a quality end product, it is necessary to cook meat to the tender stage before dehydrating. Raw meat is tough and chewy and is used to make jerky. Use any cooked left-over meat available to prepare for campouts and convenience foods. After the meat is cool, remove all fat, cube or slice it to the desired size, then place it in the dehydrator and dry it. Store in an air-tight container at 40° F.

Meat Spreads

Ham (160A)

- 2 cups diced or ground ham chunks
- ¾ cup water
- ½ cup mayonnaise
- 1 tsp prepared mustard

Rehydrate ham by soaking in water for 20 minutes. Add mayonnaise blended with the mustard. Mix well and use for a sandwich filling.

Beef (160B)

- 2 cups ground cooked beef (left-over roast)
- 1 cup buttermilk or water
- 2 Tbsp mayonnaise
- Dash pepper
- ½ cup chopped sweet pickle

Rehydrate beef in buttermilk or water for 10 to 15 minutes. Add mayonnaise, pepper and sweet pickle. Mix well. Serve on crackers, a sandwich, or it may also be used to stuff celery. A hard-boiled egg grated into the mixture is also good.

Tuna (160C)

- 1 cup dehydrated tuna
- ½ cup water
- 2 Tbsp mayonnaise
- 1 Tbsp pickle relish

Reconstitute tuna in water for 15 minutes. Add mayonnaise and pickle relish. Mix well and serve.

Turkey (160D)

- 2 cups dehydrated ground turkey
- ¾ cup boiling water
- ½ cup finely diced celery
- ¼ cup minced onion
- ½ tsp salt
- Dash cayenne pepper
- 2 hard-cooked eggs, chopped
- 1 Tbsp lemon juice
- ¼ tsp pepper
- ¾ cup mayonnaise

Reconstitute turkey in boiling water for 15 minutes. Combine ingredients, mixing well. Can be covered and refrigerated for several hours to allow flavors to blend.

Chicken (160E)

- 1 cup dehydrated ground chicken
- ⅜ cup boiling water
- 2 Tbsp finely chopped onion
- 3 Tbsp finely chopped celery
- Mayonnaise to taste
- Salt and pepper

Reconstitute chicken in boiling water for 15 minutes. Combine other ingredients, mix well and spread on sandwich. Garnish with alfalfa or radish sprouts.

Curried Meat Balls and Apricots (161)

- 1 lb ground beef
- 1 tsp salt
- ⅛ tsp pepper
- 3 Tbsp vegetable oil
- 1 cup finely chopped onion
- 1 tsp curry powder
- 1 tsp honey
- 2 cups beef broth
- 1 cup dried apricot slices
- 1 Tbsp cornstarch
- 3 cups cooked rice

Mix beef with salt and pepper. Shape into 16 one-inch meat balls. Brown the meat balls in 2 tablespoons of the oil. Remove browned meat balls and add the remaining tablespoon of oil, the onion, and brown. Add the curry powder and cook, stirring constantly about 2 minutes. Stir in the honey, 1¾ cups broth, apricots, meat balls, and bring to a boil. Turn heat down, cover pan, and simmer 15 minutes. Mix cornstarch with the other ¼ cup broth. Stir sauce in skillet and cook for a few seconds. Serve curried meat balls with hot, cooked rice. Makes 4 servings.

Meat Loaf (162)

- 1¼ lbs ground round
- 1 egg
- ½ cup finely crushed bread crumbs (see recipe #53)
- 1 Tbsp horseradish
- 2 tsp honey
- 1½ tsp salt
- 1 Tbsp dehydrated onion
- 3 Tbsp catsup
- 1 cup plain yogurt

Mix together all ingredients except yogurt. Then add yogurt and blend in carefully. Place in an ungreased 9 x 5 x 3-inch pan. Top with additional catsup and sweet basil if desired. Bake at 350° F. for 1 hour.

Tomato-Rich Meat Loaf (163)

- 1¼ lbs ground beef
- ¾ cup instant nonfat dry milk
- ⅔ cup crushed branflakes*
- ⅔ cup catsup
- 1 Tbsp dehydrated onion
- ½ cup water
- 1 tsp Worcestershire sauce
- 1 tsp salt
- ¼ tsp thyme
- 1 egg, slightly beaten

Combine ground beef, nonfat dry milk, branflakes, ⅓ cup catsup and dehydrated onion; mix well. Add water and seasonings to egg and blend into meat mixture. Pat into loaf pan and spread ⅓ cup catsup on top. Bake 1 hour at 350° F. Remove to warm platter and serve.

*Use homemade bran flakes made by baking the bran washed out of gluten.

Sweetened Condensed Milk (164)

- 4 cups dry powdered milk (instant)
- 1 cup hot water
- 2 cups sugar
- 4 Tbsp margarine

Place milk and water in blender and add sugar and margarine. Mix until sugar is dissolved. Refrigerate to store. Makes 1 quart. Use in recipes that call for sweetened condensed milk. One can equals 1⅓ cups. This mixture thickens as it stands. Should be stored in refrigerator overnight before using.

Stuffed Mushroom Hors d'oeuvres (165)

- 18 button mushrooms
- 1 lemon
- 3 oz dehydrated smoked salmon
- 2 hard-boiled eggs
- ½ tsp horseradish
- 2 Tbsp whipped cream
- Black pepper

Pull out mushroom stalks and set them aside to be dehydrated for future use. Put the mushroom caps into boiling salted water seasoned with lemon juice, and cook for 1 minute. Drain and dry on paper towel. Reconstitute salmon by steaming, and remove bones and skin. Place salmon, eggs, horseradish and cream into blender and mix until creamy. Season with salt and freshly ground black pepper. Fill mushrooms with the above mixture. Place on a plate garnished with fresh parsley.

Nectarine Alaska (166)

- 6 thick slices of pound cake
- ¼ cup apple juice
- 2 cups dehydrated nectarine slices
- 3 egg whites
- ⅛ tsp cream of tartar
- 6 Tbsp sugar
- 1 pt vanilla ice cream

Reconstitute nectarine slices by steaming. Sprinkle the cake with apple juice; top with nectarines and chill. Beat egg whites with cream of tartar until foamy; gradually add sugar. Continue beating until stiff. Quickly cut ice cream into ½-inch thick slices; fit over cake. Spread meringue* over top and sides. Bake at 450° F. about 3 minutes until the meringue is browned but ice cream not melted. Serve at once.

Super Meringue* (166A)

- 1 Tbsp cornstarch
- 2 Tbsp cold water
- ½ cup boiling water
- 3 egg whites
- 6 Tbsp sugar
- Pinch of salt
- 1 tsp vanilla

Dissolve cornstarch in cold water. Stir in to boiling water. Cook, stirring until mixture boils and thickens. Cool completely. Beat egg whites at high speed with a mixer until fluffy. Gradually add sugar, salt and vanilla. Beat until the mixture is thick and glossy. Reduce the mixer speed to medium. Add cornstarch mixture gradually, beating until smooth. Spread on slightly cooled pie filling. Bake in microwave oven about 2½ minutes, turning 3 times. Bake in conventional oven at 350° F. for 20 minutes or until evenly browned. Spread meringue evenly to edge of pie, sealing thoroughly to prevent weeping.

Egg or Spinach Noodles (167)

- 2⅔ cup flour
- 4 medium eggs
- 1½ Tbsp oil
- 2 tsp salt

Place flour in a conical shape on a large pastry board. Make a hole in the middle in which to put eggs, oil and salt. Work the mixture with hands until the dough can be rolled into a ball. It may be necessary to dip fingers in warm water to work the dough. To make spinach noodles add ½ cup well-drained, finely chopped cooked spinach. Blot the spinach leaves after they are cooked with paper towels. Knead the dough about 10 minutes. When it is smooth, cover it and let it stand for 45 minutes. Divide the dough in fourths and roll 1 part at a time. Keep the remaining dough covered with a towel. Roll and stretch the dough. Add flour if necessary to prevent the dough from sticking to the rolling pin or the board. Repeat the rolling and stretching until the dough is paper-thin. Sprinkle flour lightly on top of the rolled dough, and roll up the dough as for a jelly roll. With a sharp, thin knife, cut into strips ¼-inch (soup) to 2 inches (lasagne) as desired. Sprinkle with flour and shake out strips. Place on the dehydrator tray to dry at 145° F. for 20 minutes.

A noodle attachment for mixers or a noodle maker speeds the time of making noodles. When the dough is mixed to the ball stage, it can then be kneaded and formed with the machine. When the dough is at the smooth stage, it can be put through the noodle press of the mixer to be formed into noodles. With a little more work, they can be made by hand. However they are made, fresh noodles are second to none.

Place in a plastic bag until ready to cook and keep refrigerated. Make a double batch and freeze half for future use or as a convenience. Cook the noodles in rapidly boiling, salted, oiled water about 10 minutes. Drain and serve.

Onion (General Instructions) (168)

"And the tears flowed like wine"—ever heard that before? Does that happen when onions are being prepared for dehydration? What is the secret? How about a pair of onion-cutting goggles available at the gourmet shops! When preparing the onion, peel off the skin layers, but leave ½ inch of the root end intact. There is a mild stimulating oil at the root end, and when onions are cut it forms a vapor that affects nerves in the nose that are connected to the eyes and tears flow. Use a sharp knife and keep the head up. Do not bend over the onions and inhale the vapors. If a large quantity of onions are cut to dry at one time, save the juice and use it in cold dishes, hot sauces or dressings for flavoring.

Orange-Pear Sauce (169)

- 1/4 cup sugar
- 1 1/3 Tbsp cornstarch
- 1/4 tsp salt
- 1/8 tsp cinnamon
- 1 1/2 Tbsp maple syrup
- 1 cup orange juice
- 1 Tbsp butter
- 2 oranges, sectioned
- 1 cup dehydrated pear slices, cubed (rehydrate by steaming)

In medium pan, mix sugar, cornstarch, salt, cinnamon, maple syrup and orange juice. Cook over medium heat, stirring constantly, until the mixture thickens and comes to a boil. Simmer 1 minute. Stir in butter, orange sections and pear cubes. Heat until butter melts. Serve hot over pancakes.

Candied Papaya (170)

Cut papaya in half lengthwise. Scoop out and discard seeds. Peel and slice in 3/8-inch strips.

- 2 cups peeled, sliced papaya
- 2 cups sugar
- 1 cup water

Place 1 cup sugar and water in a frying pan and bring to a boil. Place the sliced papaya into the syrup mixture. Turn heat down and simmer for 10 minutes. Remove from heat and allow to stand 12 hours. Place the frying pan on the stove and turn heat to low. Holding fruit to one side carefully, add 1 cup sugar to the mixture, stirring until dissolved. Heat to boiling. Turn heat down and simmer until fruit is transparent. Lift fruit from the syrup. Drain and place in dehydrator set at 120° F. When dry, store in a tightly covered container.

Peaches (General Instructions) (171)

The Rio Oso Gem peach has a lower moisture content and will dry faster than other varieties. Freestone or clingstone peaches can be dried. The clingstone is harder to work with and there is more waste, but it has a delightful flavor when dried. Peach circles make an appealing gift pack. To make circles, cut the top slice off from the peach, remove the pit and continue slicing in 3/8-inch rings to the bottom of the peach. Both top and bottom circles will be flat. Center slices will have a hole in the middle that can be stuffed with a candied cherry when making peach upside-down cake or in decorating a gift pack of dried fruits.

Peach Bars (172)

- 1 cup peach leather pieces reconstituted in 1 cup water, pureed in blender
- ½ cup soft margarine
- ¼ cup granulated sugar
- 1⅓ cups sifted flour
- ½ tsp baking powder
- ¼ tsp salt
- 2 eggs, well beaten
- 1 cup packed brown sugar
- ½ tsp vanilla
- ½ cup slivered almonds
- Powdered sugar

Combine margarine, granulated sugar and 1 cup flour. Mix until crumbly. Pack into greased 8 × 8 × 2-inch pan. Bake at 350° F. for about 25 minutes or until lightly browned.

Sift together ⅓ cup flour, baking powder and salt. Set aside. Beat eggs and gradually add brown sugar. Add sifted flour mixture and stir well to combine. Add vanilla, nuts and peach pulp. Spread over baked layer. Continue baking 30 minutes or until done. Cool in pan. Cut into bars and roll in powdered sugar.

Cinnamon Swirl Peach Bread (173)

- 1 pkg hot roll mix
- ¾ cup very warm water (105 to 115 degrees)
- 2 tsp orange-flavored instant breakfast drink
- ½ cup chopped rehydrated peach slices (steam 3-5 minutes to soften)
- 1 egg
- ¼ cup sugar
- 1½ tsp cinnamon
- 1 Tbsp butter, melted

In a large bowl, dissolve yeast from hot roll mix in water. Stir in 1 teaspoon instant orange drink, peach and egg. Add dry mixture; blend well. Cover; let rise in dehydrator until light and doubled in size.

Grease an 8 × 4-inch loaf pan. On a well-floured surface, toss the dough until it's no longer sticky. Press or roll out the dough into a 12 × 7-inch rectangle. Combine sugar, cinnamon and 1 teaspoon instant orange drink; reserve 1½ teaspoons and sprinkle rest over dough. Starting with the shorter side, roll up tightly; seal edges. Place sealed-side down in a greased pan. Cover; let rise in warm place until light and doubled in size—45 to 60 minutes. Bake at 350° F. for 40 to 45 minutes until golden brown. Immediately remove from pan. Brush with butter; sprinkle with reserved sugar mixture.

Peach Cobbler (174)

- 1 cup sugar
- 2 tsp baking powder
- ¾ cup milk
- 1 cup flour
- ½ tsp salt
- ½ cup margarine (Melt in 9 × 13-inch pan)
- 1 tsp cinnamon
- 2½ cups peaches, rehydrated in 1¼ cups boiling water for 10 minutes
- ¼ cup sugar
- 1 tsp cinnamon

Mix sugar, baking powder, milk, flour and salt together and pour into melted margarine in pan. Sprinkle with 1 teaspoon cinnamon. Place rehydrated peaches over dough mixture. Include any remaining liquid. Mix ¼ cup sugar and cinnamon together and sprinkle over top of peaches. Bake at 350° F. for 35 to 40 minutes or until crispy.

This cobbler may be used with any fruit desired by adjusting the amount of sugar and spice and substituting the fruit used.

Rhubarb Cobbler (175)

Using recipe #174, substitute 2½ cups rhubarb for the peaches. Increase sugar to ½ cup, and omit the cinnamon.

Peach Muffins (176)

- 2 cups flour
- ⅔ cup instant nonfat dry milk crystals
- ¼ cup sugar
- 1 Tbsp baking powder
- 1 tsp salt
- ½ tsp cinnamon
- ¼ tsp nutmeg
- 1 cup finely chopped peach slices (steam to reconstitute)
- 1 egg, slightly beaten
- 1 cup water
- ¼ cup oil

Combine flour, instant milk crystals, sugar, baking powder, salt, cinnamon and nutmeg in medium bowl. Stir in peaches. Combine egg, water and oil; blend well. Pour the egg mixture over the flour mixture; stir just until blended. Do not overmix. Spoon into 16 greased 2½-inch muffin cups, filling only ⅔ full. Bake at 400° F. 20 to 25 minutes or until golden brown. Serve with creamed honey.

Whipped Creamed Honey (177)

Place one cup liquid honey into a blender and puree until light and creamy, about 4 minutes. Thick honey produces a more firm end product.

No-Crust Peach Pie (178)

Reconstitute 3 cups peach slices in 1½ cups of boiling water. Let them stand 10 minutes and then place them in a 9-inch deep-dish pie plate. Sprinkle 2 tablespoons of granulated sugar and 1 teaspoon of cinnamon over the top.

In a separate bowl, mix the following ingredients:

- 1 cup brown sugar
- 1 cup flour
- ½ teaspoon nutmeg
- ½ square margarine
- ½ teaspoon salt

Stir the above mixture with a fork until it is crumbly. Sprinkle over the top of the peaches and bake at 400° F. for 30 minutes.

Spicy Peach Salad (179)

Reconstitute 2 cups dehydrated peach slices in 1 cup boiling water. Let stand 10 minutes. Drain peach slices and set aside. Reserve water from reconstituting peaches.

- Water
- 2 Tbsp vinegar
- ¼ cup sugar
- 10 whole cloves
- 2 cinnamon sticks
- 1 3-oz pkg peach gelatin
- ⅓ cup instant nonfat dry milk crystals
- ⅓ cup ice water
- 1 Tbsp lemon juice

Add enough water to the water reserved from reconstituting the peaches to make 1 cup. Combine the 1 cup of water, vinegar, sugar, cloves, and cinnamon sticks in a saucepan. Heat to boiling; cover and simmer 10 minutes. Strain the syrup mixture over gelatin in bowl. Stir until gelatin is dissolved. Chop peaches and add to gelatin. Chill until consistency of unbeaten egg whites. Mix milk crystals and ice water in a small mixer bowl. Beat at high speed until soft peaks form—3 to 4 minutes. Add lemon juice. Continue beating until stiff peaks form. Fold into gelatin mixture. Spoon into 8 individual ½-cup molds. Chill until firm.

Peachy Banana Flip (180)

- ¼ cup dehydrated banana slices
- ½ cup dehydrated peach slices
- 2 cups milk
- 1 Tbsp sugar
- ½ tsp salt
- ½ tsp vanilla
- 1 cup plain yogurt
- 4 or 5 ice cubes, cracked

Combine banana, peach, and milk. Blend until smooth. Add sugar, salt, vanilla, yogurt and cracked ice. Blend and serve.

Peanuts (General Instructions) (181)

Peanuts are ready for harvest when the leaves turn yellow, the kernels develop and the veins in the pods darken. Lift the bush out of the ground gently and shake off the dirt. Pick up any peanuts that may have fallen off from the bush. Gather the rest of the peanuts and place them on a dehydrator tray. Dry at 110° F.

Roast peanuts in the shell. Place one layer deep on a cookie sheet in the oven at 300° F. for about 30 minutes. Check for doneness by removing a shell and letting the nut cool.

A special treat is homemade peanut butter. Use 1½ tablespoons of peanut oil and 1 cup fresh-roasted peanuts. Place oil, ⅓ teaspoon salt and a few peanuts into a blender and puree. Add the remaining nuts a few at a time.

Try sprouting raw peanuts. Hull 1 cup peanuts. If the red skin of the nut is torn, the seed will not germinate. Soak in tepid water overnight and place in sprouter. Wash 3 times a day with tepid water and drain. As soon as the sprout emerges, carefully remove the red skin and the nut is ready to be used. It is truly crisp and delicious. Use in sprout stir frys, or salads.

To maintain best eating quality, store peanuts in a cool, dry place. Vacuum-sealed nuts keep indefinitely if unopened. If peanuts are stored in a refrigerator in the shell, they will keep about 9 months. Shelled nuts keep about 3 months at refrigerator temperature.

Homemade "Cracker Jack" (Home-dried Popcorn and Peanuts) (182)

- 10 cups popped popcorn, warm
- 1½ cups peanuts
- ½ cup margarine
- 1 cup brown sugar, packed
- ¼ cup dark corn syrup
- ¼ tsp salt
- ¼ tsp soda
- ½ tsp vanilla

Mix together popped corn and peanuts in a very large bowl. Keep warm in a 250° F. oven.

Melt margarine in a heavy 2-quart pan. Stir in brown sugar, corn syrup and salt. Bring to a rolling boil, stirring constantly. Boil, without stirring, 5 minutes. Remove from heat; stir in soda and vanilla. Quickly pour over popcorn-peanut mixture, tossing until kernels and nuts are well coated. Spread out in a shallow baking pan. Bake at 250° F. for 45 minutes, stirring once or twice. Remove from the oven and pour onto aluminum foil to cool. Break into pieces and store in tightly-covered container. Should it become soft, place in the dehydrator set on 145° F. for about 30 minutes.

Peanut Butter Crunch Bars (183)

- 1 cup toasted wheat germ
- 1 cup dried skim milk
- ⅓ cup honey
- ½ cup raisins
- ¼ tsp salt
- 1 cup mixed dried fruits, chopped (steam to reconstitute)
- 3 cups crunchy peanut butter
- 1 cup toasted dehydrated grated coconut

Mix wheat germ, milk, honey, raisins, salt and dried fruit. Add enough peanut butter to make the mixture stiff but not crumbly. Roll mixture into balls, or press on flat surface by hand or with a rolling pin until it is about ½-inch thick. Cut into 1½-inch squares. Cover with grated coconut. Store in covered container in the refrigerator. Makes about 5 dozen bars. Wrap bars individually for use in back-packing as quick-energy bars.

Peanut Butter-Raisin Chews (184)

- 1 cup peanut butter
- 1 cup corn syrup
- 1½ cups instant nonfat dry milk
- 1¼ cups powdered sugar
- 1 cup monukka raisins

Mix all ingredients well. Form into balls and roll in graham cracker crumbs. Chill before serving.

Pears (General Instructions) (185)

Wash pears. To avoid grainy skins, peel and cut in half from the stem end to the blossom end. Remove the stem, blossom and core. For small pears, cut each half lengthwise into 2 pieces, parallel to the beginning cut. Cut medium to large pears into 3 pieces and extra-large pears into 4 pieces. For best results, slices should not exceed ½ inch in thickness. Dip in sodium bisulfite solution for 2 minutes, drain, and dry. Pears should be yellow but firm to maintain good color when they are dried. If pears should soften unexpectedly, they can be sulfured to help maintain a pretty color after they are dried.

Pear Bread (186)

- ⅓ cup butter
- 1 cup sugar
- 1 egg, well beaten
- 2½ cups sifted flour
- 4 tsp baking powder
- ¾ tsp pumpkin pie spice
- ½ tsp salt
- 1 cup milk
- ¼ cup flour
- 4 cups dehydrated pear slices, reconstituted by steaming 5 minutes

Cream butter and sugar together. Add egg; beat lightly. Sift together 2½ cups flour, baking powder, pumpkin pie spice, and salt. Add dry ingredients to creamed mixture alternately with milk, beating after each addition. Dredge pears in remaining ¼ cup flour; add to batter. Pour into greased, floured 8 × 4 × 3-inch bread pan. Bake at 375° F. for 40 to 45 minutes or until done.

Pear Almond Cake (187)

- 6 cups dehydrated pear slices reconstituted by steaming
- ½ cup cookie crumbs
- 2 Tbsp butter
- ½ cup butter
- ½ cup sugar
- 2 egg yolks
- ½ cup blanched almonds, ground
- ½ tsp almond extract
- ½ tsp grated lemon rind
- 3 Tbsp lemon juice
- 3 egg whites

Place reconstituted pears in a greased 10-inch pie plate. Sprinkle with crumbs and dot with 2 tablespoons butter. Cream butter with sugar until smooth. Add egg yolks, one at a time, beating until light and fluffy. Stir in almonds, extract, lemon rind and juice. Whip egg whites until stiff. Fold into egg yolk mixture. Spread over pears and bake at 375° F. about 30 minutes or until golden brown. Cool partially, serve warm with ice cream.

Pear Bread Pudding (188)

- 3 cups dehydrated pear slices reconstituted by adding 2 cups boiling water. Let stand 10 minutes
- 3 eggs, beaten
- 1½ cups milk
- 2 tsp lemon juice
- 1 tsp vanilla
- 1 slice whole wheat bread, cubed
- ½ cup raisins
- ⅔ cup sugar
- ¾ teaspoon cinnamon
- ¼ tsp ginger

Dice pears, drain and reserve liquid. Combine liquid with eggs, milk, lemon juice, and vanilla in large mixing bowl. Fold in bread cubes and raisins.

In a small bowl, combine the sugar, cinnamon and ginger, reserving 1 tablespoon. Add the sugar mixture to the pudding and pour it into a 10 × 6 × 1½-inch baking dish. Sprinkle with 1 tablespoon sugar mixture. Place baking dish in a shallow pan of hot water to a depth of 1 inch. Bake at 350° F. for 40 minutes or until set.

Persimmons (General Instructions) **(189)**

Persimmons reconstitute better if sliced, but some people like them whole. To dry whole persimmons it takes about 30 hours. Crystals of sugar will form on the outside. When this occurs, knead the fruit to redistribute the moisture and permit further drying. Continue to knead the fruit every few hours and this will speed the drying time and also give a more appealing end product. The Hachiya is the best variety for drying whole.

The Fuyu persimmon is crisp, like an apple, and can be peeled with a vegetable peeler. It can be cut in slices and dehydrated or it can be cut in circles whichever is preferred.

Granola Persimmon Cookies (190)

- 1 cup persimmon puree
- 1½ cups flour
- 1 cup sugar
- ½ tsp baking soda
- 1 tsp salt
- 1¼ tsp pumpkin pie spice
- ¾ cup shortening
- 1 egg, well beaten
- 1¾ cups granola
- ½ cup chopped nuts
- 1 tsp vanilla

Reconstitute 1 cup persimmons with enough boiling water to cover and blend to a smooth puree.

Sift the dry ingredients. Cut in shortening. Add egg, persimmon, granola, nuts and vanilla. Stir thoroughly. Drop by teaspoonfuls, about 1½ inches apart onto an ungreased cookie sheet. Bake at 400° F. about 11 minutes or until lightly browned. Cool on rack.

Persimmon Cookies (191)

- 1½ cups dried persimmons reconstituted in 1¾ cups hot water
- 1 Tbsp dried lemon peel
- 1½ cups sugar or 1 cup honey
- 2½ cups flour
- ½ tsp salt
- 1 cube margarine
- ½ cup sugar
- 1 tsp baking powder

Puree persimmons, lemon peel and sugar or honey in blender. Combine flour, salt margarine, sugar and baking powder; mix together until crumbly. Pat approximately 2 cups of this mixture into the bottom of a 9 x 13-inch pan (reserve the remaining mix for the top crust). Pour persimmon mixture over dough—spread evenly. Sprinkle the reserved crumbs on top. Bake at 350° F. for 15 minutes, or until lightly browned.

Crisp Persimmon Pie (192)

- 1½ Tbsp tapioca
- ½ cup sugar
- 1 tsp grated orange peel
- ¼ tsp cinnamon
- 2 Tbsp lemon juice
- 6 cups dehydrated sliced Fuyu persimmons reconstituted by steaming for 3 minutes
- Pastry for a 2-crust 9-inch pie

Combine tapioca with sugar; stir in orange peel, cinnamon, lemon juice and persimmons, mixing gently until blended. Let stand 15 minutes. Stir before placing in a pastry-lined pan. Cover with top crust, seal and flute edge. Make vents in top crust. Bake at 375° F. for 40 to 50 minutes or until pastry is browned and filling is bubbling. This pie is very rich so cut small serving pieces.

Steamed Persimmon Pudding (193)

- 1 cup dehydrated persimmons
- 1¼ cups flour
- 1½ tsp soda
- ½ tsp salt
- 1½ tsp baking powder
- 1 cup sugar
- ½ cup soft bread crumbs
- 1 cup raisins
- 1 cup chopped nuts
- 1 tsp vanilla
- 1½ tsp margarine
- ½ cup milk

Reconstitute persimmons in a 1-cup measure by adding boiling water to cover; puree.

Sift dry ingredients. Add remaining ingredients. Mix thoroughly. Spoon into a greased 1½-quart pudding mold; cover mold. Steam in covered kettle with boiling water half way up the side of the mold for 3 hours. Good served with lemon sauce (see recipe #158).

Steamed puddings may be sliced into ½-inch thick pieces and dehydrated. To reconstitute just place in a steamer and steam for 10 minutes. This is not recommended for long-time storage but is ideal to mail to someone away from home.

Persimmon Roll (194)

- 1 cup dehydrated persimmons
- ½ cup chopped nuts
- 10 dates, pitted and chopped
- ½ cup maraschino cherries
- ½ cup dehydrated shredded coconut
- 1 cup miniature marshmallows
- ½ cup chopped figs
- 4 cups graham cracker crumbs

Reconstitute persimmons in boiling water to the one-cup measure and blend until smooth.

Mix all ingredients together and place on waxed paper (which has been sprinkled with graham cracker crumbs). Form into a 2-inch roll (diameter). Wrap in waxed paper and chill in the refrigerator for 3 hours. Slice and serve with whipped topping (see recipe #286) that has been seasoned with ½ teaspoon pumpkin pie spice.

Natural Fruit Pie Glaze (Microwave) **(195)**

- 1 cup dried fruit
- 1½ cups boiling water
- 1 cup white corn syrup

Place fruit and water in a glass dish in the microwave. Cook on high for 3 minutes or until it comes to a boil. Reduce setting to simmer and continue cooking for 10 minutes. Cool slightly and puree in a blender until smooth. Press through a fine sieve and measure ½ cup puree, add corn syrup and place in the microwave and boil rapidly for 3 minutes or until mixture is clear. This is enough glaze for one 9-inch pie. Choose the fruit used in the pie to make the glaze. Cool thoroughly before adding the reconstituted fruit.

Use any surplus puree to flavor yogurt.

Pineapple Bars (196)

- ½ cup margarine
- 2 Tbsp honey
- ½ cup date or brown sugar
- ½ tsp vanilla
- ½ cup chopped, dehydrated pineapple
- 1 cup whole wheat pastry flour
- ½ tsp salt
- ¾ cup oatmeal (quick cooking)
- ½ cup wheat germ
- ½ cup dehydrated grated coconut
- ½ cup chopped nuts
- ¾ cup carob chips

Cream the margarine, honey, and sugar. Add vanilla and pineapple and blend. Add flour and salt and mix well. Add oatmeal, wheat germ and mix well. Blend in remaining ingredients. Bake on a greased 13 × 9-inch baking pan at 350° F. for 25 minutes, or until edges are browned. Cool thoroughly. Cut into 2-inch squares.

To rehydrate pineapple, measure ½ cup chopped leather, add boiling water to just cover and let soften (about 5 minutes).

Pineapple Date Bread (197)

- 2 cups flour
- ¼ cup light-brown sugar packed
- 3 tsp baking powder
- 1 tsp salt
- 1 cup chopped, dehydrated pineapple
- 1 cup chopped, pitted dates
- 1 cup chopped pecans
- 2 eggs
- ⅔ cup milk
- ¼ cup oil

Reconstitute pineapple by adding boiling water to cover. Let stand until soft (about 5 minutes).

Stir together flour, sugar, baking powder and salt. In a small pan cook the pineapple with liquid and dates over low heat, stirring constantly until the liquid is absorbed and mixture is thick. Stir in nuts. Cool about 10 minutes.

Combine eggs, milk and oil; add date mixture and stir until smooth. Add liquid ingredients to the flour mixture, just until flour is moistened. Pour into a greased, paper-lined 8½ x 4½-inch loaf pan. Bake at 350° F. for 1 hour. Cover with foil the last 15 minutes to prevent over browning. Cool in pan.

Candied Pineapple (White Sugar) (198)

Both canned or fresh pineapple can be used in making candied pineapple. There is a difference in flavor and color.

Cut off the top and bottom slice from a fresh pineapple. Remove the eyes and trim out the core. Slice in 3/8-inch circles.

- 2 cups prepared pineapple (dry slices with paper towel)
- 2 cups sugar
- 1 cup water

Place 1 cup sugar and water in a frying pan and bring it to a boil. Place the pineapple into the syrup mixture. Turn the heat down and simmer for 10 minutes. Remove from heat and allow to stand 12 hours. Place the frying pan on the stove and turn heat to low. Holding fruit to one side, carefully add 1 cup of sugar to mixture, stirring until dissolved. Heat to boiling. Turn heat down and simmer until fruit is transparent. Lift fruit from syrup. After the fruit is saturated, it is ready to be dried. Drain and place on trays to dry. Put on a solid sheet to prevent it from dripping into the bottom of the dehydrator. Dry at 120° F. Store with wax paper separators in a tightly covered container.

Save the excess syrup to be used for waffles or pancakes.

Candied Pineapple (Brown Sugar) (199)

2 cups pineapple (tidbits)
½ cup brown sugar

Cut pineapple in tidbit-size pieces. Place 2 cups of pineapple in a pan and add ¼ cup brown sugar. Simmer for 10 minutes. Let stand for 12 hours. Add ¼ cup brown sugar to the 2 cups of pineapple tidbits and repeat the simmering process for 10 minutes. Let stand for 12 hours. The third time do not add sugar, but just simmer the pineapple for 10 minutes. Let it stand for 12 hours and drain. Place in the dehydrator to dry. It will remain sticky but is delicious. Dry at 120° F.

Pineapple Milk Shake (200)

1 cup pineapple leather pieces
Water
1 pt milk
1 Tbsp lemon juice
4 scoops vanilla ice cream
Pineapple sherbet

Place 1 cup of broken pieces of dehydrated pineapple leather in blender. Add water to the 1-cup measure and let stand for 5 minutes to soften. Add milk and lemon juice. Puree until smooth. Add vanilla ice cream and blend. Add 1 scoop pineapple sherbet to each glass before serving.

Pineapple Ricotta Pancakes (201)

2 cups chopped, dehydrated pineapple leather
¼ cup flour
1 tsp baking powder
Pinch of salt
1 tsp wheat germ
4 extra large eggs, beaten
1 cup ricotta cheese
⅔ cup milk
½ tsp vanilla
1 cup whipping cream

Reconstitute pineapple by adding boiling water to just cover and soaking until soft. The pineapple should only be as moist as drained crushed pineapple.

Stir together flour, baking powder, salt and wheat germ. Add eggs and ricotta; mix well. Stir in milk, vanilla and half the pineapple. Bake on lightly greased griddle over moderately low heat, using about 2 tablespoons batter for each pancake. Turn and cook second side. Keep warm while cooking remaining pancakes. Beat cream just until stiff and fold in remaining pineapple. Serve pancakes topped with the pineapple-cream. Makes 24 three-inch pancakes.

Quick Pineapple Rolls (202)

- 1 cup chopped, dehydrated pineapple
- ½ cup soft butter
- ½ cup brown sugar, packed
- 1 tsp cinnamon
- 1 can refrigerator biscuits

Reconstitute pineapple by adding boiling water to just cover and soak until soft, about 5 minutes.

Add butter, brown sugar and cinnamon. Mix well. Spoon into 10 large muffin cups (well greased). Open a can of refrigerator biscuits; place a biscuit in each cup over pineapple mixture. Bake 10 minutes at 425° F. Let cool 5 minutes, then invert to remove from pan.

Pineapple-Strawberry Pie (203)

- 1 8-oz can crushed pineapple
- 1 cup cream cheese, softened
- ½ tsp vanilla
- 2 cups strawberry pie filling*
- ¼ cup confectioners' sugar
- 1 cup heavy cream
- 1 9-inch graham cracker pie crust

Drain pineapple well, reserving two tablespoons of syrup. Combine softened cream cheese, vanilla and reserved syrup, mixing until well blended. Stir in ¼ cup pineapple and ½ cup pie filling. Gradually add sugar to cream, beating until soft peaks form. Fold into cream cheese mixture. Pour into crust. Top with remaining pineapple and pie filling. Chill until firm.

*Reconstitute 2 cups of dehydrated strawberry slices by steaming. Fold into commercially-prepared glaze.

Pineapple-Zucchini Cake (204)

- 3 eggs
- 2 cups sugar
- 2 tsp vanilla
- 1 cup oil
- 2 cups dehydrated grated zucchini
- 3 cups flour
- 1 tsp baking powder
- 1 tsp salt
- 1 tsp soda
- ½ cup raisins
- 1 cup nuts
- 1 cup rehydrated crushed pineapple

Put the zucchini into the blender and add boiling water to the two-cup measure. Puree until smooth.

To reconstitute the pineapple, fill a cup with broken pieces of chopped, dehydrated leather and add boiling water to cover. Let stand (about 5 minutes) until soft. For even reconstitution, stir several times with a fork.

Beat eggs until fluffy. Add sugar, vanilla, oil, zucchini, flour, baking powder, salt, and soda. Mix well. Then add raisins, nuts and pineapple. Pour into two 4 x 7½-inch loaf pans and bake at 325° F. for 1 hour.

Pizza Dough (205)

- ½ tsp active dry yeast
- ¾ cup plus 2 Tbsp warm water
- 3 cups flour
- Dash of salt

Dissolve the yeast in water. Measure flour by dipping method. Blend in flour. Knead on lightly-floured surface. Place in a greased bowl, and turn it to grease the top. Cover and let rise in a warm place until double.

Divide in half and press into pans. Add sauce, cheese, etc. Bake in 425° F. oven 12 to 15 minutes. Makes two 14-inch pizzas.

Peggy's Pizza Sauce (206)

- 1 tsp dehydrated onion
- 1½ cups dehydrated tomatoes reconstituted in 1½ cups water
- 1 tsp salt
- 1 tsp sugar (optional)
- 1 tsp mixed Italian seasoning
- Dash of pepper
- ½ cup Bran (optional, makes a thicker sauce)

Mix in blender, add one bay leaf, and refrigerate overnight. Use 1⅓ cups pizza sauce on each pizza; remove the bay leaf before using.

Zucchini may also be added to the sauce for a more nutritional sauce. Just add ½ cup of grated dehydrated zucchini and ½ cup of water and blend with the tomatoes.

Dehydrated Pizza Sauce (206A)

This sauce can be dehydrated for short-time storage. Spices go rancid in long-time storage.

- 4 cups tomatoes
- ½ small onion
- 1 tsp salt
- 1 tsp sugar (optional)
- 1 tsp mixed Italian seasoning
- Dash of pepper

Puree tomatoes and add remaining ingredients. When sauce is smooth, pour onto a glass pizza plate lined with plastic wrap and make a round pizza filling. Makes two pizzas. When it is dry, roll and store it on the shelf. For long-time storage, place in the freezer. To reconstitute, make the dough, roll out the sauce on top of the dough, and sprinkle with about ½ cup of water to rehydrate it. Let it stand for 10 minutes and then build up cheese, etc.

Dehydrated mushrooms have to be rehydrated in boiling water for 5 minutes before placing them on pizzas or they will be too dry. There isn't enough moisture on pizza to reconstitute the mushroom. Reconstitute the mushrooms in the water, drain them, and use the same water to reconstitute the pizza sauce for additional flavor and nutritional value.

Plum Cake (207)

- 1½ cups chopped reconstituted purple prune plums
- 1 cup granulated sugar
- ½ cup brown sugar
- ¾ cup oil
- 1 egg, beaten
- 1 tsp grated orange peel
- 2 cups flour
- ¼ tsp salt
- 1 tsp soda
- 1 cup buttermilk
- Nut topping

Steam and chop plums to measure 1½ cups. In a mixing bowl blend the sugars, oil, egg and orange peel. Sift together the flour, salt and soda. Add to the sugar mixture alternately with buttermilk, stirring well after each addition. Stir in plums. Pour into a greased 9 x 13-inch baking pan. Sprinkle with Nut Topping.* Bake at 350° F. for 35 minutes, or until the cake tests done. Serve with whipped cream, if desired.

Nut Topping

- ¼ cup sugar
- ¼ cup chopped walnuts
- 1 tsp cinnamon

Combine ingredients. Toss to mix thoroughly. Sprinkle over cake batter.

Plum Dumplings (208)

- 3 cups fruit juice
- ¾ cup sugar
- 2 cups biscuit mix
- ⅔ cup milk
- 12 rehydrated plum halves (steamed to rehydrate)
- 1 Tbsp lemon juice
- ½ cup melted butter
- 1 cup brown sugar

Mix the juice and sugar in a saucepan. Bring to boil; simmer 5 minutes. Set aside. Mix the biscuit mix and milk with a fork. Turn onto a well-floured board and knead 5 times. Pat out to ½-inch thickness. Cut into 12 squares. Put rehydrated plum half on each square. Pinch closed and roll into a round ball. Lower one at a time into simmering syrup; cook 3 minutes. Turn the dumpling over, cover the pan and simmer 5 minutes more. Remove with a slotted spoon to serving plates. Drizzle lemon juice over the dumplings, then butter. Sprinkle with brown sugar. Serve warm with fruit syrup. Serves 6.

Popcorn (General Instructions) **(209)**

Popcorn must be dried on the cob. Leave the ears on the stalks until fully ripe. Then remove the ears, husk them, and place them in a large muslin bag and hang them to dry. Protect them from rodents when drying on screens. The corn may be stored on the cob, but to save space it should be shelled and stored in a moisture-proof container. To shell the corn, hold the cob in both hands and twist in opposite directions. Have a container available to catch the falling kernels. It may be necessary to wind-blow the corn to remove cob chaff.

Potato (General Instructions) **(210)**

Have you ever tasted home-made potato chips? They're delightful! Do not try to dehydrate potato granules for making mashed potatoes. The commercial granules are made with sophisticated equipment that produces a quality product. When a potato is steam blanched, the starch granules swell and absorb water (steam), resulting in a sticky, pasty, potato. If a potato is not pretreated, it will turn black. Pretreatment with sodium bisulfite is the best method of pretreatment for a quality product. Slice the potato very thin for potato chips, a little thicker for escalloped potatoes and fried potatoes. Potatoes can also be sliced for french fries, and grated for hash browns. Dip the potatoes in to the solution and soak them for 2 minutes. Drain and dry. It is not necessary to peel new potatoes. Just scrub thoroughly and slice.

Sweet Potatoes (210A)

Sweet potatoes can also be pretreated by dipping in sodium bisulfite. Just slice in 3/8-inch slices after they are thoroughly scrubbed and dry. They do not have as long a storage life when they are dipped. To retain carotene, they should be steam blanched until tender and then dried. (Sweet potatoes may also be pretreated in a microwave. Refer to instructions for microwave pretreatment.)

Yams—Use the same pretreatment for yams as for sweet potatoes.

Potato Chips (210B)

Use dehydrated potatoes that have been cut no more than 1/16-inch thick. Place in bowl and cover with boiling water. Let stand 10 minutes while grease in a deep-fat cooker is heating. Drain on an absorbent towel. Deep fry until golden brown, sprinkle with seasoned salt and serve.

Potato Soup (211)

- 3 small onions quartered
- 2 Tbsp margarine
- 4 cups dehydrated potato slices
- 3 Tbsp chopped celery
- 2 cups water
- 1 tsp salt
- 4 cups half-and-half
- 1 cup diced cooked ham

Saute onions in margarine until soft but not brown. Add potatoes, celery and water. Simmer until reconstituted and tender, about 15 minutes. Cool slightly and puree in blender. Add salt to half-and-half and heat, but do not boil. Add puree from blender and the diced, cooked ham. Serves 6.

Two-Potato Soup (Microwave) (212)

- 1 cup dehydrated sweet potato slices
- 1 cup dehydrated potato slices
- ½ tsp basil
- ⅛ tsp white pepper
- 1 Tbsp chicken base
- 1 Tbsp dehydrated onion
- 1 cup half-and-half
- ½ cup sour cream
- 4 Tbsp crisply cooked crumbled bacon
- Parsley, snipped

Place 2 cups of potato slices in a 4-cup measure and add water to the 2 cup level. Cook on high for 1 minute. Place in a blender and puree. Add basil, pepper, chicken base and onion. Puree until smooth. Heat half-and-half, but do not boil. Combine the puree, half-and-half and sour cream. Reheat, if necessary. Garnish with crumbled bacon and snipped parsley.

Potpourris and Sachets (General Instructions) (213)

Potpourris are made from coarse broken pieces of herbs, spices and flowers, and placed in a decorative jar with a tight-fitting lid. Sachets are composed of powdered herbs, spices and flowers and sewn into small decorated fabric bags to be placed in a drawer of clothing or in a closet.

A fixative is a plant material used to fix or set and hold the fragrance. The most common and available fixative is orris root. The root is dried and stored for a time before being ground into powder. It has a delicate but distinct odor of violet.

Gather herbs and petals and place them in a dehydrator at 100° F. to dry. When the herbs are dry, remove the leaves from the stem. Use glass containers and wooden spoons when working with herbs. Mix the herbs, flower petals and fixative and place them in a tight-sealing container. Store in a dark, cool place and allow the mixture to blend and fix the scent. Do not use plants that have been sprayed with chemicals. Stir the mixture once a week for several weeks before completing the project. Flower petals dried in silica gel maintain a better color.

To make potpourris, use the coarsely-broken herbs, spices and flowers. To make sachets, the flowers must be crushed to a fine powder and the spices and citrus peels must be finely ground. Use a mortar and pestle or a blender to powder the mixture.

Lemon Verbena (213A)

- 2 cups verbena leaves
- 1 cup thyme
- 1 cup lemon peel
- 1 cup marigold petals for color
- 2 Tbsp orris root
- 1 tsp cinnamon
- 1 tsp allspice

Use a large wooden spoon to stir together the ingredients. Mix thoroughly. Place in a wide-mouthed jar and place lid on tightly. Keep in a dark, cool place and stir once a week. When the scent is fixed, bottle the potpourri. Grind the mixture and sew into small pillows to make sachets.

Rose-Geranium (213B)

- 3 cups rose geranium leaves
- ½ cup mint geranium, lime geranium and apple geranium
- 1 cup rose petals
- 1 cup red geranium petals
- 2 Tbsp orris root

Stir together and mix. Store until the scent is fixed and prepare potpourris or sachets.

Sweet Marjoram and Basil (213C)

- 1½ cups dried rose petals
- ½ cup white carnation petals
- 1 Tbsp (a few leaves) each of thyme, rosemary, sweet marjoram, and basil
- 3 bay leaves, crushed
- 1 tsp allspice
- ¾ tsp anise seed
- 3 Tbsp each tangerine and lemon rind, grated and dried
- 3 Tbsp orris root

Mix well. Let stand until scent is fixed. Bottle or powder to make sachets.

Visit the local thrift store and collect interesting jars, jugs, or bottles with tight-fitting lids. Decorate them with yarn, ribbon, decals, or paint designs with acrylic paints. Potpourris and sachets make lovely gifts. Remnant laces, braids and rickrack purchased at the yardage shop can be used to decorate sachets.

Christmas Prune Cake (214)

- ¾ cup oil
- 1 cup sugar
- 2 eggs
- 1¾ cups flour
- 2 tsp baking powder
- 1 tsp soda
- 1 tsp cinnamon
- ½ tsp cloves
- ½ tsp salt
- 1½ cups reconstituted prunes
- ¾ cup chopped walnuts

Place prunes in a blender and fill with hot water to the 1½-cup level. Puree until smooth.

Cream together the oil, sugar, and eggs. Mix the dry ingredients and add alternately with prunes. When well blended, add nuts. Pour into 2 well-greased and floured 4 × 7½-inch loaf pans. Bake at 350° F. for 30 minutes. While still warm, drizzle powdered sugar frosting until it runs down the sides. Decorate with maraschino cherries, gum drops, and nut halves. This can be baked in smaller pans and used as presents.

Country Prune Bread (215)

- 56 medium prune halves
- Milk
- 1 egg slightly beaten
- 3 cups biscuit mix
- ¼ cup melted margarine
- ½ cup sugar
- 1 tsp cinnamon
- ½ cup chopped nutmeats

Cook prune halves. Add enough milk to beaten egg to make ¾ cup and mix. Stir into biscuit mix. Knead slightly; roll out on a lightly floured board to 12 × 21-inch oblong. Cut into 28 3-inch squares. Place 2 prune halves in center of each; bring up corners over prune; pinch together to form a ball. Dip each ball in melted margarine, then in mixed sugar and cinnamon. Arrange 8 balls close together in 2 rows in a greased 9 × 5 × 3-inch loaf pan; sprinkle with a third of the nuts. Top with 12 balls in 3 rows, pressing lightly on others; sprinkle with a third of the nuts. On top, press 8 balls in 2 rows and top with the rest of the nuts. Bake at 375° F. for 45 to 55 minutes. Let stand in pan 10 minutes before removing. Slices best after 24 hours.

Prune-Plum Coconut Balls (216)

- ¾ cup dried French prune-plums reconstituted by steaming
- ½ cup pecans
- ½ tsp dried grated orange rind
- ½ tsp dried grated lemon rind
- ¾ cup dehydrated grated coconut
- 1 Tbsp lemon juice

Reconstitute French prune-plums by steaming. Grind French prune-plums and pecans in a food chopper with a medium blade. Combine with remaining ingredients. Mix well. Shape into small balls 1¼ inch in diameter.

Pumpkin Bread (217)

- 2/3 cup shortening
- 2 2/3 cups sugar
- 4 eggs
- 2 cups dehydrated pumpkin leather
- 2/3 cup water
- 3 1/3 cups flour
- 1/2 tsp baking powder
- 2 tsp soda
- 1 1/2 tsp salt
- 2 tsp pumpkin pie spice
- 2/3 cup chopped nuts
- 2/3 cup dates, finely chopped

To reconstitute the pumpkin leather, place 2 cups of broken pieces of leather in a blender. Add boiling water to the 2-cup measure. Allow to stand 5 minutes, add the 2/3 cup water from recipe, and blend the pumpkin and water to a smooth puree.

Cream shortening and sugar. Add eggs and pumpkin. Sift together flour, baking powder, soda, salt, and spice. Add to the pumpkin mixture. Stir in nuts and dates. Pour into two 2-quart greased loaf pans. Bake at 350° F. for 1 hour, or until done.

Pumpkin Cake (218)

- 1/2 cup shortening
- 1 cup brown sugar, packed
- 1 egg
- 1/2 cup sugar
- 3/4 cup buttermilk
- 2 1/4 cups flour
- 3 tsp baking powder
- 1/2 tsp salt
- 1/4 tsp soda
- 1 1/2 tsp cinnamon
- 1/2 tsp ginger
- 1/2 tsp allspice
- 3/4 cup reconstituted pumpkin
- 1/2 cup finely chopped walnuts
- 1/2 cup chopped dates

Reconstitute pumpkin leather by placing 3/4 cup of broken pieces in a cup and adding water to the 3/4 measure. Puree in a blender to a smooth consistency.

Cream together shortening and brown sugar. Add egg and sugar and cream mixture. Measure and sift dry ingredients. Add buttermilk and flour mixture alternately. Stir in pumpkin, walnuts and dates. Pour into greased 8 x 16-inch loaf pan. Bake at 350° F. for 30 to 35 minutes. Serve warm with a dollop of whipped cream.

Pumpkin Cake Roll (219)

- 3/4 cup flour
- 1 tsp baking powder
- 2 tsp cinnamon
- 1/2 tsp salt
- 1 tsp ginger
- 1/2 tsp nutmeg
- 3 eggs
- 1 cup sugar
- 2/3 cup rehydrated pumpkin leather
- 1 tsp lemon juice
- 1 cup finely chopped walnuts
- Powdered sugar

Reconstitute the leather by placing ⅔ cup of pumpkin leather pieces in the blender and adding boiling water to the ⅔ cup measure. Blend until smooth.

Sift together dry ingredients and set aside. Beat eggs five minutes or until very thick. Gradually beat in 1 cup of sugar. Add pumpkin and lemon juice to the egg mixture. Fold in the dry ingredients. Spread in a well-greased and floured jelly roll pan. Sprinkle the top with finely chopped nuts. Bake at 375° F. for 15 minutes. Loosen the edges and turn out immediately onto a dish towel sprinkled with powdered sugar. Starting at the narrow end, roll the towel and cake together. Cool and unroll. Spread with filling. Roll and chill before slicing to serve.

Filling

- 1 cup powdered sugar
- 4 Tbsp butter
- 1 6-oz package cream cheese
- ½ tsp vanilla

Beat together until creamy.

Pumpkin-Chocolate Cookies (220)

- ½ cup margarine
- 1½ cups sugar
- 1 egg
- 1 cup rehydrated pumpkin leather
- 1 tsp vanilla
- 2½ cups flour
- 1 tsp baking powder
- 1 tsp baking soda
- ½ tsp salt
- 2 tsp pumpkin pie spice
- ½ cup slivered almonds
- 1 cup chocolate chips

Place 1 cup broken pumpkin leather in a blender, add boiling water to the 1-cup measure. Let stand 5 minutes and puree until smooth.

Cream margarine and sugar together until light and fluffy. Beat in egg, reconstituted pumpkin and vanilla. Mix and sift flour, baking powder, baking soda, salt, and pumpkin pie spice. Add to creamed mixture; mix well. Add almonds and chocolate chips; mix thoroughly. Drop by teaspoonfuls onto well-greased cookie sheets. Bake at 350° F. for 15 minutes or until lightly browned. Cool on racks. Yields 6 dozen cookies.

Pumpkin Cookies (Filled Center) (221)

- ¾ cup shortening
- ½ cup brown sugar, packed
- 1 egg
- ¼ cup light molasses
- 1 cup quick oats
- 2 cups flour
- ½ tsp baking soda
- 1 tsp salt
- 1 recipe pumpkin filling

Cream shortening and sugar. Beat in egg and molasses. Place the oats in a blender container. Cover. Blend until finely chopped. Mix oats, flour, soda and salt. Stir into creamed mixture. Cover. Chill.

On a floured surface roll dough 1/8-inch thick. Cut into 36 3-inch circles. Place 1 teaspoon of pumpkin filling on top of half of the circles. Place on ungreased cookie sheet. Cut jack-o-lantern faces in remaining circles or leave them plain to resemble pumpkins. Place on top of filling. Seal edges, press stems out from dough scraps. Bake at 375° F. for 12 minutes. Makes 18.

Pumpkin Filling

- ½ cup pumpkin reconstituted
- ½ cup sugar
- 1¼ tsp pumpkin pie spice

To reconstitute pumpkin place in blender with boiling water added to the ½ cup measure. Let stand for 5 minutes and then puree to smooth consistency. Add other ingredients and puree until well blended.

Pumpkin Doughnuts (222)

- 2 eggs, beaten
- 1 cup sugar
- 1 cup dehydrated pumpkin leather
- 2 Tbsp melted butter
- ¼ cup milk
- 3 cups flour
- 2 tsp baking powder
- 1 tsp cinnamon
- ½ tsp allspice
- ½ tsp ginger
- ½ tsp nutmeg
- ½ tsp salt

To reconstitute pumpkin leather, fill to the 1-cup level with broken pieces of leather and cover with boiling water. Let stand 5 minutes and puree until smooth.

Beat eggs, add sugar, pumpkin, butter, milk, and dry ingredients. Fry at 385° F. Makes about 3 dozen doughnuts. This is especially good when frosted with caramel frosting.

Caramel Frosting (222A)

- ½ cup packed brown sugar
- ¼ cup milk
- 3 Tbsp margarine
- ¾ tsp vanilla
- ¾ to 1 cup powdered sugar

Combine brown sugar, milk and margarine in a small pan. Heat until the sugar dissolves; cool slightly. Stir in vanilla. Gradually add powdered sugar; beat until smooth.

Pumpkin Freeze (223)

- 20 vanilla wafers
- 1 pint vanilla ice cream
- 2 cups pumpkin leather
- 1 cup hot water
- Evaporated milk
- 1 cup sugar
- ½ tsp salt
- 1 Tbsp pumpkin pie spice
- 1 tsp vanilla
- 1 cup whipped cream

Line a 10-inch pie plate with vanilla wafers. Spread ice cream over cookies. Freeze until firm.

Place pumpkin leather in a blender. Add hot water and let stand for 5 minutes. Puree until smooth. Add enough evaporated milk to make 2 cups of pureed pumpkin. Add sugar, salt, pumpkin pie spice and vanilla. Fold 1 cup of whipped cream into this mixture. Pour into pie shell. Cover with foil and freeze until firm—about 3½ hours.

Remove pie from freezer 15 minutes before serving. Whip ½ cup cream. Decorate top with cream and caramelized almonds (see recipe #4).

Pumpkin-Lentil Soup Amandine (224)

- ¼ cup butter or margarine
- 2 large onions, chopped
- ½ cup lentils
- 5 cups chicken stock
- 1½ cups rehydrated pumpkin
- ⅛ tsp marjoram
- ⅛ tsp thyme
- ¼ tsp coarsely ground pepper
- Dash of Tabasco sauce
- 1 cup half-and-half
- Salt to taste
- ½ cup toasted sliced almonds

Place broken pieces of pumpkin leather in cup and add boiling water to cover. Let stand for 5 minutes.

Melt butter or margarine in a large pan; add onions and cook until lightly browned. Stir in lentils and chicken stock. Add pumpkin. Crush herbs and add to soup along with pepper and Tabasco sauce. Simmer about 1½ hours or until lentils are done. Let cool, then puree in blender. At serving time, heat to simmering; add half-and-half and salt. Pour into soup bowls or cups and top with almonds. Serves 6.

Pumpkin-Nut Muffins (225)

- 1 cup corn meal
- ½ cup sifted flour
- 2½ tsp baking powder
- ¾ tsp salt
- ⅓ cup sugar
- ½ tsp cinnamon
- ¼ tsp ginger
- ⅛ tsp cloves
- ¼ cup chopped pecans
- ½ cup raisins
- 1 cup pumpkin leather
- 1 egg, beaten
- ⅔ cup milk
- ¼ cup vegetable oil
- Confectioners' sugar frosting
- 48 candy corns

To puree leather, place 1 cup broken pieces in a blender and add enough boiling water to make 1 cup. Let stand 5 minutes and puree until smooth.

Sift together flour, baking powder, salt, sugar, cinnamon, ginger and cloves into a medium bowl. Stir in pecans, corn meal, and raisins. Add pureed pumpkin, egg, milk, and oil. Stir only until dry ingredients are moistened. Fill greased muffin cups ⅔ full. Bake in a 425° F. oven for 20 to 25 minutes or until golden brown.

Glaze muffins with thin confectioners' sugar frosting and arrange 4 candy corns on each. Serve warm with butter. Makes 12 muffins.

Pumpkin Pancakes (226)

- 1 cup pancake mix
- ¾ cup milk
- 1 egg
- ¼ cup rehydrated pumpkin
- 1 Tbsp Safflower oil
- ¼ tsp cinnamon
- ⅛ tsp nutmeg

Reconstitute pumpkin by placing ¼ cup pumpkin in blender and adding boiling water to the ¼-cup measure. Puree until smooth.

Place mix, milk, egg, pumpkin, oil, cinnamon and nutmeg in a bowl. Stir lightly until the batter is fairly smooth. Pour about ¼ cup of batter onto a hot, lightly greased griddle and brown. When tops are covered with tiny bubbles, it is time to turn the pancake and brown on the other side. Don't turn too soon. Serve with whipped butter.

Whipped Butter (226A)

- 2 tsp unflavored gelatin
- 1 cup milk
- ½ pound butter
- ½ tsp salt
- 2 drops of yellow food coloring

Soften gelatin in 2 Tablespoons of the milk; dissolve by placing gelatin in a bowl and placing that bowl in a pan of hot water. Cool to room temperature. Cut butter into small pieces and heat over hot water until soft enough to beat (but not melted—on a warm day, room temperature is fine). Add dissolved gelatin and salt to the remaining milk. With an electric mixer, gradually whip this mixture into the butter. When milk is entirely absorbed, a few drops of yellow food coloring may be added, if desired. If the milk separates from the butter, chill for a few minutes and whip again. Place in a plastic margarine tub with a tight-fitting lid and keep covered in the refrigerator until hard.

Do not use whipped butter to grease baking pans or to fry foods.

Pumpkin Pecan Pie (227)

- 4 cups pumpkin leather
- 1 cup powdered creamer
- 6 eggs
- 1½ cups light brown sugar
- ½ cup dark corn syrup
- 1 tsp salt
- 3½ tsp pumpkin pie spice
- 1½ cups boiling water
- 2 unbaked 9-inch pie shells
- 1 Tbsp butter, melted
- ½ cup chopped pecans
- ½ cup whole pecans, for garnish

Break 4 cups of pumpkin leather into a blender and add boiling water to the 4-cup measure. Let stand 5 minutes. Puree until smooth.

In a large bowl combine pumpkin, powdered creamer, eggs, sugar, syrup, salt and spice. Beat until well blended. Add boiling water gradually. Mix well. Brush bottom of pie shells with melted butter. Sprinkle chopped pecans over the bottom of the pie shells. Pour filling into the pie shells. Bake at 350° F. for 55-60 minutes, or until a knife inserted in the center comes out clean. Garnish with reserved pecans; cool and slice.

Pumpkin Pie (228)

- 2 cups pumpkin leather
- 3 eggs
- 1 cup sugar
- 1 tsp salt
- 2 tsp pumpkin pie spice
- 1 can evaporated milk
- 1 9″ unbaked pie shell

Break pumpkin leather into pieces and place in blender. Add water to the 2-cup measure, cover and let stand while assembling other ingredients. Puree until smooth. Add all other ingredients to the leather in the blender. Blend to a thick custard-consistency. Pour into an unbaked 9-inch pie shell. Bake at 425° F. for 15 minutes; reduce heat to 350° F. for another 45 minutes. The pie is done when a knife inserted into the center comes out clean. Cool and serve with whipped cream.

Banana squash leather or dehydrated slices may be substituted by reconstituting in the same manner as with pumpkin. Measure 2 cups of slices, add boiling water to the 2-cup measure, let stand 5 minutes and puree.

Pumpkin Seeds (General Instructions) (229)

Scoop seeds out of the center of the pumpkin. Remove the fibrous tissue. Place the seeds on a teflex sheet and place in a dehydrator at 110° F. until they are crisp. Remove hulls and season. Place 1 tablespoon of oil (for each cup of seeds) into a heavy frypan and place over high heat. Add seeds and stir continuously to prevent scorching. When they are lightly browned, place on a paper towel and sprinkle with ¼ teaspoon salt for each cup of seeds.

Pumpkin Wheat Muffins (230)

- 2 cups whole wheat flour
- 2½ tsp baking powder
- 1 tsp salt
- ¼ cup shelled, untoasted pumpkin seeds
- 1 egg, beaten
- ¾ cup milk
- ⅓ cup oil
- ⅓ cup molasses

Stir together flour, baking powder, and salt. Add chopped pumpkin seeds. Beat together egg and milk; blend in oil and molasses and stir into dry ingredients just until blended. Pour batter into well-greased muffin tins, filling each about ⅔ full. Bake 20 to 25 minutes at 400° *F. Makes 12 muffins.*

Raisin Corn Crunch (231)

- 10 cups popped corn
- 4 cups bite-size shredded wheat cereal
- 2 cups Monukka raisins
- 2 cups walnuts, chopped coarsely
- ½ cup butter
- 1 cup sugar
- ½ cup light molasses
- 1 Tbsp grated orange peel or 1 tsp dehydrated orange peel
- 2 tsp cinnamon
- ½ tsp salt
- 2 tsp orange extract

Combine popped corn, cereal, raisins and walnuts in a large, buttered bowl. Combine butter, sugar, molasses, orange peel, cinnamon, and salt in a heavy pan; bring to boil over medium heat, stirring constantly; boil about five minutes. Stir in extract. Pour over popped corn mixture; stir quickly to coat well. Press firmly into two greased jelly roll pans, pressing the top level. Let stand several hours. Cut into 2-inch squares.

Raisin Fruitcake (232)

- 2 cups monukka raisins
- 2 cups golden raisins
- 1 cup sliced dried apricots steamed
- 1 cup slivered almonds blanched
- 1 cup chopped walnuts
- 1 cup halved candied cherries
- 2 cups diced candied pineapple
- 2½ cups diced candied fruits and peels
- 1¼ cups shortening
- 1¼ cups honey
- 6 eggs
- 2½ cups flour
- 1 tsp baking powder
- 1¼ tsp salt
- 1 tsp cinnamon
- ½ tsp cloves

Combine raisins, apricots, nuts, candied fruits and peels. Cream shortening and honey together. Beat in eggs one at a time. Sift flour with baking powder, salt and spices. Blend into batter. Stir in fruits and nuts, mixing well. Turn into a greased 10-inch tube pan lined with 2 thicknesses of greased brown paper and one of waxed paper. Bake at 250° F. about 5 hours. Place a shallow pan of hot water on the bottom of the oven.

Raisin Rice Krispie Confection (233)

- ½ cup corn syrup
- ½ cup peanut butter
- ½ cup raisins
- 1½ cups sifted confectioners' sugar
- 3 to 4 cups Rice Krispies

Blend corn syrup, peanut butter, raisins and sugar thoroughly. Add 2 cups of the Rice Krispies; mix until well blended. Shape firmly into balls about 1-inch in diameter. Roll the balls in the remaining Rice Krispies, pressing them lightly into the surface. Let stand in a cool place to harden. Makes about 32 balls.

This recipe may be varied by using dehydrated apple chunks, apricot bits, nectarine pieces, peaches, pears, etc. (steamed to reconstitute).

Raspberry Freeze (234)

- ¼ cup honey
- 1 cup softened cream cheese
- 1½ cups dehydrated raspberries
- 1 cup boiling water
- 1 cup heavy cream, whipped
- 2 cups miniature marshmallows

Reconstitute raspberries in boiling water and blend until smooth. Press through fine sieve to remove seeds.

Add honey to softened cream cheese. Mix well. Stir in fruit, fold in marshmallows and whipped cream. Pour into a 9-inch square pan. Freeze. Place in refrigerator 30 minutes before serving.

Raspberry Marshmallow Pie (235)

- 1 envelope unflavored gelatin
- ½ cup cold water
- 1¼ cups rehydrated raspberries reconstituted by steaming
- ¾ cup sugar
- 1 tsp lemon juice
- 1 cup cream cheese
- ½ cup heavy cream, whipped
- 2 cups marshmallows
- 1 9-inch graham cracker crust, chilled

Soften the gelatin in cold water; stir over low heat until dissolved. Cool. Crush raspberries; stir in sugar, lemon juice and gelatin. Gradually add to softened cream cheese. Chill until slightly thickened, fold in whipped cream and marshmallows. Pour into crust; chill until firm. Serves 8.

Raspberry Bavarian (236)

- 1½ cups dehydrated raspberries
- ¾ cup boiling water
- 2 envelopes unflavored gelatin
- 2½ cups milk
- ½ cup sugar
- ⅛ tsp salt
- 2 egg yolks, slightly beaten
- 1 cup heavy cream, whipped

Reconstitute raspberries in boiling water and blend until smooth. Measure puree and add water to make 1½ cups. Soften the gelatin in cold milk. Add sugar, salt and eggs in a pan. Heat just to boiling; do not boil. Stir in raspberry puree and chill until slightly thickened. Fold in whipped cream. Turn into a 6-cup mold. Chill until firm. Unmold and serve. Makes 6-8 servings.

Raspberry Pie (237)

- 1⅞ cups boiling water
- 1 cup cold water
- 1 5-oz Junket Danish Dessert and Pie Filling* (currant-raspberry-strawberry)
- 1½ cups dehydrated raspberries
- ¼ cup sugar
- 1 9-inch pastry shell, graham cracker crust or individual tart shells
- Whipped cream

Reconstitute raspberries by steaming for 3 minutes until they are soft.

Heat 1-7/8 cups of water to boiling. Never use milk. Add cold water to Junket; mix well, stirring until the mixture is smooth. Add the mixture to the boiling water, stirring constantly until it boils. Remove from the heat. Add sugar to raspberries and stir into mixture. Pour the mixture into a baked 9-inch pastry shell. Sprinkle the surface lightly with sugar while it is warm to keep the surface moist. Refrigerate for 3 hours before serving. Garnish with whipped cream just before serving.

*Salad Foods, Inc.

Minute Brown Rice (General Instructions) (238)

- 2 cups brown rice
- 5 cups water
- 1 tsp salt

Bring water to a boil. Add salt. Slowly add rice. Cover and simmer over low heat for 40 minutes or until all of the water has been absorbed.

Place rice in dehydrator to dry. It will take approximately 10-12 hours.

To reconstitute, add 1 cup boiling water to 1⅓ cups rice. Let stand 10 minutes and prepare as required for recipe.

Minute White Rice (General Instructions) **(238A)**

- 2 cups white rice
- 4 cups water
- ½ tsp salt

Slowly stir rice into vigorously boiling salted water. Shake the pan to make sure the rice is evenly distributed. Cover and turn heat to low. Simmer about 25 minutes or until water has been absorbed. Salt added to the water keeps the kernels separated.

Place rice in dehydrator to dry. It will take approximately 10-12 hours.

To reconstitute, add 1 cup boiling water to 1⅓ cups rice. Let stand 5 minutes and prepare as required for recipe.

This is excellent for a quick meal. Reconstitute the rice while making up beef stroganoff sauce.

Quick Stroganoff (Microwave) **(239)**

- 2 cups cubed, cooked roast beef trimmed
- ½ Tbsp dehydrated onion
- ¼ cup margarine
- 2 Tbsp whole wheat flour
- ½ cup dehydrated mushrooms
- 2 cups beef stock
- ¼ tsp seasoned salt
- ¼ tsp pepper
- ¼ tsp garlic salt
- 1 tsp salt
- 1 cup sour cream
- 2 Tbsp fresh parsley
- 1⅓ cups rice
- 1 cup boiling water

Combine all ingredients except parsley, sour cream, rice and water in a 2-quart glass casserole. Cook on reheat for 5 minutes covered. Stir and continue cooking until hot. Remove from the oven and let stand 5 minutes. Place rice and boiling water in a 1-quart casserole and simmer for 3 minutes. Stir the sour cream into the meat sauce. Place parsley around edge of rice casserole and dinner is ready.

Minute Brown Rice (Microwave) **(240)**

Choose a 3-quart glass cooking dish with a lid. Bring 3 cups of water to a boil on high. Stir in 1 cup of brown rice and set the oven on simmer. Cook covered for 25 minutes; stir after 5 minutes. Remove rice from the oven and let stand for 5 minutes. Remove the lid and place rice in a dehydrator to dry. Stir the rice several times during the drying time to break up the kernels. One-half teaspoon of salt added to the cooking water will help keep the kernels separate.

To reconstitute brown rice, add 1 cup boiling water to 1⅓ cups rice. Let stand 10 minutes and prepare as required for recipe.

Brown rice retains its germ and bran coat, but is slow to tenderize. Long-grain types are best for salads, soups and main dishes. Short-grain types cook up tender and moist and are used in recipes for puddings, sauces and rings.

Minute White Rice (Microwave) **(240A)**

White rice may also be precooked. Choose a 2-quart glass cooking dish with a lid. Bring 2 cups of water to a boil on high. Slowly stir in 1 cup of white rice. Set oven for simmer and cook for 15 minutes, stirring after 5 minutes. Remove rice from the oven and let stand for 5 minutes. Remove the lid and place the rice in a dehydrator to dry. Rice cooked without salt will require stirring several times during the drying time to break up the kernels.

To reconstitute white rice, add 1 cup boiling water to 1⅓ cups rice. Let stand 5 minutes and it is ready to use.

Rice prepared in advance can be a time saver in an emergency. It can also be used in any recipe calling for cooked rice.

Spanish Rice (Microwave) **(241)**

- 2 Tbsp margarine
- ¼ cup chopped green pepper
- 2 cups stewed tomatoes
- 1 Tbsp dehydrated onion
- 2 cups minute rice plus
- 1 cup boiling water to reconstitute
- ½ tsp leaf basil

Place margarine and green pepper in a 2-quart glass casserole. Microwave on medium for 4 minutes or until pepper is partly cooked. Add remaining ingredients, mixing well. Cover with a lid or plastic wrap and cook on reheat for 3 minutes. Stir and break up tomatoes by cutting through them. Recover and continue to cook on reheat until hot. Let stand, covered, 5 minutes so rice absorbs juices from tomatoes. Serves 4.

Rice and Eggs Au Gratin **(242)**

- 1⅓ cups minute white rice
- ¼ cup chopped chives
- 2 Tbsp butter
- 6 eggs beaten
- 1½ cups grated Cheddar cheese
- ¾ tsp dry mustard
- ¼ cup milk

Prepare rice. To half of the rice, add chives and butter. Place in casserole dish and keep warm. Beat eggs. Add grated Cheddar cheese, the remaining rice, and dry mustard blended with milk. Scramble in melted butter till the eggs are done but still soft. Spread over rice in casserole. Serves 6.

Sage Dressing (243)

- 2 medium onions
- Bacon drippings
- 3 cups finely ground dried bread
- 1 Tbsp dehydrated sage leaves rubbed
- Hot liquid from giblets
- Salt and pepper to taste

Sautee onions in bacon drippings until brown. Mix well with bread. Add sage leaves. Moisten to desired consistency with hot liquid from giblets. The giblets may also be chopped fine and added to the mixture. Add salt and pepper to taste. Bake at 350° F. for 25 minutes.

Sage Gravy (244)

- 1 cup boiling water
- 1 Tbsp dehydrated onion
- 2 Tbsp butter
- 1 Tbsp beef base
- 1 tsp dehydrated sage leaves, rubbed
- Salt and pepper
- 1 Tbsp flour

Place water in a pan and bring to a boil. Add onion, butter, beef base, sage, salt and pepper. Thicken with flour. Simmer for 10 minutes. Serve over reheated sliced turkey, chicken, or meat loaf.

Basic White Sauce (245)

This is a thin sauce like half-and-half and is used for cream soups and vegetables.

- 1 Tbsp butter
- 1 Tbsp flour
- ¼ tsp salt
- 1 cup milk

Medium White Sauce (246)

This is a medium sauce like heavy cream and is used for scalloped dishes.

- 2 Tbsp butter
- 2 Tbsp flour
- ¼ tsp salt
- 1 cup milk

Thick White Sauce (247)

This is a thick sauce like batter for croquettes and souffles.

- 4 Tbsp butter
- 4 Tbsp flour
- ¼ tsp salt
- 1 cup milk

Melt butter in a small pan. Add flour and salt and stir to a smooth paste. Cook 1 minute to avoid floury taste. Remove from heat and add half of the milk, stirring until blended. Return to heat and stir constantly until the mixture begins to thicken. Add remaining milk. Heat to simmering and cook 5 minutes. If too much milk evaporates while cooking, the sauce will be doughy.

Chunky Sauces (General Instructions) **(248)**

All of the "No Cook Butter" recipes may be made into chunky sauces in the same way as the Chunky Apple Sauce. Just use dehydrated slices in the blender. Increase the water to ¾ cup and do not puree, but chop to the consistency desired.

Chunky Apple Sauce

2	cups dehydrated apple slices	⅓	cup sugar
¾	cup hot water	1	tsp cinnamon
		1	tsp lemon juice

Put apple slices in the blender. Add hot water and let stand for 5 minutes. Add sugar, cinnamon and lemon juice and chop until ingredients are thoroughly mixed but still chunky. Place in a covered jar in the refrigerator over night so that the apple chunks will soften. It is then ready to serve.

Seasoning Salt (General Instructions) **(249)**

For people who grow and dry their own herbs, this is a money saver. Make a jar with Italian seasonings, Mexican seasonings, French seasonings, etc. It is more convenient to have just one jar of spices than to have to get spices from several jars.

1	cup salt	1½	tsp oregano
2½	tsp paprika	1	tsp garlic powder
2	tsp dry mustard	½	tsp onion powder

Combine all ingredients, mixing well and store in an airtight container. Makes 1-1/8 cups. Do not use additional salt in recipes without first tasting. This is good used to season meats, fish, vegetables, and salad dressings.

These flavors are good on chicken, pot roast, lamb, fish and salads.

¾	cup salt	1	tsp marjoram
1	tsp thyme	1	tsp garlic powder
4	tsp paprika	¾	tsp curry powder
1	tsp dry mustard	1	tsp onion powder
½	tsp dill weed	1	tsp celery salt

Combine all ingredients, blending together very well. Store in airtight containers. Makes about 3 cups.

Shepherd's Pie (Microwave) **(250)**

- 2 cups dehydrated roast beef, ground
- 1 cup dehydrated mushrooms
- 1½ Tbsp beef base
- 1 cup water
- 1 Tbsp freshly chopped chives
- 1 Tbsp butter
- 1 Tbsp flour
- Salt and pepper
- 3 cups mashed potatoes
- Parsley

Reconstitute roast beef by adding boiling water to cover. To the mushrooms add ½ cup boiling water. Let meat and mushrooms stand 5 minutes.

Place the beef base, water, chives and butter in a 2½-quart microwave dish. Bring to a boil and thicken with flour, stirring every 30 seconds until thick. Add meat, mushrooms, and soaking water. Season with salt and pepper. Smoothly cover with mashed potatoes, dot with butter and bake in a microwave uncovered on high for 20 minutes. Let stand 5 minutes, garnish with fresh parsley and serve.

To make the pie in the conventional oven, place the ingredients in a pan and thicken. Then pour into an oven casserole, place potatoes on top and bake at 350° F. for 30 minutes. Remove and garnish with fresh parsley and serve.

This recipe can also be made with 1 cup ground gluten and 1 cup ground beef. Mix the ground gluten and beef with ¾ cup water, add mushrooms and then follow the directions as above.

Smoked Salmon and Egg Salad (251)

- 2 cups reconstituted smoked salmon
- 1 lemon
- Cayenne pepper
- 4 hard-boiled eggs, chopped
- Mayonnaise
- Lettuce
- Watercress
- Tomato wedges

Break salmon into fine pieces and steam for 5 minutes to reconstitute. Remove large bones and skin. Blend chopped salmon and lemon juice with a shake of cayenne pepper. Lightly toss chopped egg, salmon, and enough mayonnaise to bind together. Arrange on a bed of lettuce. Garnish with watercress and tomato wedges.

Salmon Loaf (Microwave) (252)

- 2 cups dehydrated salmon reconstituted by steaming
- 2 eggs
- 1½ cups milk
- 1 cup coarsely crushed cracker crumbs
- 2 Tbsp chopped onion
- 2 Tbsp lemon juice
- ¼ tsp salt
- ¼ tsp pepper
- Cucumber Sauce

Remove bones and skin from salmon and flake meat. Beat eggs until foamy. Add milk. Mix in crumbs, onion, lemon juice, salt and pepper. Stir in salmon; lightly blend until moistened. Spoon mixture into a 9 x 5-inch glass loaf pan. Microwave for 10 minutes on high or until the sauce begins to set, rotating the dish one-half turn after 5 minutes. Let stand 3 to 5 minutes before serving.

Cucumber Sauce (253)

- ½ cup sour cream
- ½ cup dehydrated cucumber leather
- 2 green onions, finely chopped
- 2 Tbsp half-and-half

Reconstitute cucumber leather by measuring broken pieces of leather into a cup and filling with boiling water. Let stand 5 minutes. Puree until smooth.

Combine all ingredients; mix until blended. Serve warm or cold over slices of salmon loaf. If served warm, micro-cook about 1 minute.

Smoked Nuts (254)

- 4 cups nuts
- 1 Tbsp honey
- ¼ tsp liquid smoke
- ¾ cup water
- 1 Tbsp salt

Marinate for 45 minutes. Drain, place in a dehydrator and dry. It requires about 4 hours.

This is good with walnuts, pecans and almonds.

Smoked Salmon Quiche (255)

- 2 Tbsp butter or margarine
- 1 large tomato, chopped
- 1 smoked salmon, diced and rehydrated in ½ cup water
- 2 Tbsp minced onion
- 1 cup grated Swiss cheese
- 1 Tbsp flour
- 1 unbaked 10-inch pie shell
- 4 eggs
- 1 cup half-and-half
- ½ tsp salt
- Pepper

In a skillet, heat butter and saute tomato until mushy. Cool. Stir in rehydrated and broken salmon (remove outside skin and any large bones) and onion. Mix cheese and flour. Sprinkle cheese into shell. Spoon the salmon mixture over the cheese. In a bowl, beat eggs with half-and-half, salt and pepper. Pour mixture evenly over salmon. Bake at 350° F. for 40 to 45 minutes or until puffed and brown. Garnish with half slices of tomato.

Smoked Salmon Spread (256)

- 1 cup smoked salmon
- 1 Tbsp lemon juice
- 2 tsp grated onion
- 2 tsp horseradish
- Salt and pepper
- 1 cup cream cheese, softened
- ¼ cup chopped pecans
- 2 Tbsp snipped parsley

Break salmon into fine pieces. Reconstitute by steaming for 5 minutes. Remove large bones and skin. Combine salmon, lemon juice, onion, horseradish, salt and pepper with cream cheese. Blend together well. Shape into a ball or log on waxed paper. Wrap and chill 3 hours. Combine nuts and parsley on waxed paper. Roll salmon mold in this mixture and return to the refrigerator. Just before serving, garnish with additional parsley and serve with Wheat Snack Crackers (see recipe #294).

Sour Cream (General Instructions) (257)

- 1 pint half-and-half
- 2 Tbsp cultured buttermilk

Heat half-and-half until just barely lukewarm. Stir in buttermilk. Place in a jar with a tight-fitting lid. Shake gently about 1 minute. Set the jar in a warm place and do not disturb until it sets. This may take up to 24 hours, depending upon the temperature. This makes 1 pint of sour cream. Store in the refrigerator. It will stay fresh 3 to 4 weeks.

Spaghetti Sauce (258)

- 2 Tbsp olive oil
- 1 Tbsp dehydrated onion chopped
- 1 clove garlic, mashed
- 1 lb ground beef
- Dash of fresh-ground pepper
- 2 cups tomato slices reconstituted in 2 cups boiling water; puree until smooth
- 1 tsp salt
- 1 tsp Italian Seasoning

In 1 tablespoon oil, saute onion and garlic in a frying pan until soft. Add the ground beef, mincing as it browns. Drain off excess fat. Add tomato, seasonings and 1 tablespoon oil. Bring to a boil. Cover and simmer 20 minutes, stirring occasionally.

Cook spaghetti and drain. Serve topped with meat sauce and sprinkled with fresh-grated Parmesan cheese. Serves 6.

Spiced Nuts (259)

- 4 cups nuts
- ½ tsp cinnamon
- ¾ cup water
- ¼ cup honey
- ½ tsp nutmeg
- 1 Tbsp salt

Marinate for 45 minutes. They will require 5-6 hours to dry because of the added honey. Good with walnuts, pecans, and almonds. Set the dehydrator for 145° F. Place directly onto trays at the bottom of the dehydrator so they will not drip onto other foods in the dehydrator.

Strawberry Delight (260)

- 1 cup milk
- 1 cup cottage cheese
- ½ cup dehydrated strawberry slices
- ¼ tsp fresh lemon juice

Puree in a blender and pour into serving dishes. Add 1 teaspoon of date sugar (see recipe #97) to each dish; chill and serve.

Any dehydrated fruit may be used in place of the strawberry, however more tart fruits may require more sugar.

D.D.'s Strawberry Leather Surprise (261)

Cut strawberry leather rolls into wedge-shaped pieces. About 2½ inches at the wide end and cut to a point. Use a 4-inch length. Place ¼ teaspoon orange yogurt at the wide end and roll up in jelly-roll fashion. This makes a bite-size, tangy hors d'oeuvre.

This can not be made up ahead or the leather becomes too soft and sticky.

Strawberry-Lime Dessert (262)

- 2 cups dehydrated strawberries reconstituted by steaming
- ¾ cup boiling water
- 2 Tbsp lime juice
- 1 envelope unflavored gelatin softened in ¼ cup cold water
- 1 cup unflavored yogurt
- ¼ cup sugar
- 3 lime slices, halved

Place strawberries and water into a blender container and blend until pureed. Strain the berries through a fine sieve; discard seeds. Return to blender container and add lime juice and gelatin. Blend well until the gelatin is dissolved. Add yogurt and sugar, blending just until combined. Pour into serving dishes, chill until set. Garnish each serving with a lime slice. Serves 6.

Strawberry Pie (263)

- 1 pkg strawberry gelatin
- 1 cup boiling water
- 1 cup cold water
- 1 Tbsp sugar
- 1½ cup dried strawberries reconstituted by steaming
- 1 baked pastry or crumb crust
- ½ pint whipping cream

Dissolve gelatin in boiling water; add cold water and chill until very thick. Sprinkle sugar over berries. Add fruit to thickened gelatin and pour into a pastry shell. Allow to set 4 hours or overnight. Garnish with sweetened whipped cream, or 1 cup of whipping cream and ¼ cup sour cream.

Frozen Strawberry Yogurt (264)

- 1½ cups dehydrated strawberries reconstituted by steaming
- ¼ cup sugar
- ½ cup light corn syrup
- 2 cups plain yogurt

Place strawberries, sugar and corn syrup in the container of an electric blender. Process until smooth. Add yogurt. Blend at medium speed until combined. Pour the mixture into a 9×5×3-inch metal loaf pan. Freeze until firm, about 3 hours.

Process in a blender at medium speed until soft. Return to loaf pan. Cover and freeze until firm.

To serve as a soft-frozen dessert, stir occasionally during the second period of freezing and serve before it gets solidly frozen. After the dessert is solidly frozen, allow it to stand at room temperature about 10 minutes before serving. Makes 1½ pints.

Sunflower Seeds (General Instructions) (265)

Sunflowers can be harvested as soon as the backs of the seed heads are brown and dry. The inner rows are ripe, but need to be dried. To harvest, cut off the heads, leaving about a foot of the stock, and tie the stalks together. Hang in a protected area to dry. When thoroughly dry, remove the seeds by lightly rubbing the heads. If the dehydrator is large enough to accommodate the heads, they can be placed on a tray and dried at 100° F. Remove the stock when drying in the dehydrator. It may even be necessary to cut the head in half.

To roast, spread the seeds on a cookie sheet and heat in a 250° F. oven for 10 to 15 minutes, stirring frequently. Do not over cook—they become more crisp as they cool.

Sunflower seeds should be hulled before eating or using in recipes.

Sunflower Snack Mix (266)

- 1 cup carob chips
- 1 cup almonds
- 1 cup sunflower seeds
- 1 cup monukka raisins

Combine all ingredients and place in a compote for snacks.

Sunflower Yogurt Dip (267)

- ¾ cup sunflower seeds
- ¼ tsp salt
- 1 cup yogurt
- Dash of garlic salt
- 3 Tbsp chopped chives

Toast sunflower seeds lightly in an oven. Grind into medium pieces and mix with other ingredients. Serve as a dip for dehydrated vegetable chips.

Sweet Potato Casserole (268)

- 4 cups dehydrated sweet potatoes reconstituted
- ⅓ cup butter
- 2 Tbsp sugar
- 2 eggs, beaten
- ½ cup milk
- ⅓ cup chopped pecans
- ⅓ cup dried, grated coconut
- ⅓ cup brown sugar
- 2 Tbsp flour
- 2 Tbsp butter, melted

Reconstitute sweet potatoes by placing them in a blender and adding boiling water to the 4-cup measure. Soak 5 minutes and puree until smooth.

Mix sweet potatoes, ⅓ cup butter and sugar; beat in eggs and milk. Pour mixture into a 2-quart casserole. Combine pecans, coconut, brown sugar and flour; stir in melted butter. Sprinkle mixture over sweet potatoes. Bake at 325° F. for 1 hour.

Sweet Potatoes in Orange Shells (269)

- 8 half orange shells
- 1/4 cup honey
- 1/4 cup butter, melted
- 3/4 cup instant nonfat dry milk
- 1/2 cup orange juice
- 4 cups rehydrated sweet potatoes
- 4 Tbsp chopped pecans

Reconstitute sweet potatoes by placing 4 cups of potatoes into a blender and adding boiling water to the 4-cup measure. Let stand 5 minutes and puree until smooth.

Cut oranges in half and remove the flesh and membranes. Mix honey, melted butter, nonfat dry milk and orange juice. Add sweet potatoes and blend. Pile in orange shells and sprinkle with pecans and brush with melted butter. Bake 20 to 30 minutes. Serves 8.

Sweet Potato Pan Rolls (270)

- 2/3 cup warm water (105° to 115°)
- 2 pkgs active dry yeast
- 2 Tbsp sugar
- 1 1/2 tsp salt
- 2 Tbsp margarine
- 1 1/4 cups rehydrated sweet potatoes or yams
- 3/4 cup monukka raisins
- 3 to 3 1/2 cups flour

To reconstitute sweet potatoes, place 1 1/4 cups loosely-packed sweet potatoes into a blender. Add boiling water to the 1 1/4-cup measure. Allow to stand for 5 minutes and puree until smooth.

Measure warm water into a large warm bowl. Sprinkle in yeast; stir until dissolved. Add sugar, salt and margarine. Blend in sweet potatoes, then stir in raisins and 2 cups of the flour. Add enough additional flour to make a stiff dough. Turn out onto a lightly floured board; knead until smooth and elastic, about 8 to 10 minutes. Place in a greased bowl, turning to grease the top. Cover; let rise in a dehydrator until doubled in bulk. Punch dough down; turn out onto a lightly floured board. Divide the dough in half; divide each half into 12 equal pieces. Shape each piece into a smooth round ball. Arrange in 2 greased 8-inch round cake pans. Cover; let rise in a dehydrator until doubled in bulk. Bake at 375° F. about 25 minutes. Makes 2 dozen.

Taco Salad (271)

Layer ingredients in this order:

- Corn chips
- Shredded lettuce
- Chili beans with meat
- Grated cheese
- Dehydrated tomato slices
- Chopped onions
- Top with sour cream

Place ingredients in a Tupperware Cold Cut Keeper or a 9 x 13-inch oblong pan with a lid. (Aluminum foil or plastic wrap may also be used for a cover.) The moisture from the salad will reconstitute the tomato slices, but the salad should be refrigerated for several hours to allow for equalization of moisture.

Arrowroot Thickener (272)

Arrowroot has a neutral flavor and does not have to be cooked like flour and cornstarch. It thickens at a lower temperature and so is good to use in egg and yogurt sauces which should not be boiled. Use about 2½ teaspoons of arrowroot per cup of liquid to thicken.

Cornstarch Thickener (273)

Cornstarch is used to thicken a sauce that requires a translucent appearance. It should always be dissolved with a little cold water or liquid from the recipe before being added to the hot liquid. One tablespoon of cornstarch will thicken 1½ to 2 cups of liquid. At altitudes of 5,000 feet or above, cornstarch must be cooked over direct heat or it will not thicken. In recipes with high sugar content, it is best to thicken the liquid from the recipe and then add the sugar gradually. If the sauce thins, it could be caused from overbeating.

Gelatin Thickener (274)

Unflavored gelatin must be softened and then dissolved before it can be used. Sprinkle, do not dump the granules over the liquid. It is important for each grain to absorb the liquid, plump up and become soft enough to dissolve quickly. Sprinkle 1 tablespoon of the granules over ¼ cup cold water and let it soak 2 or 3 minutes. Combine 1¾ cups hot liquid (just at the boiling point) with the soaked gelatin and stir until dissolved.

There is 1 tablespoon of unflavored gelatin in an individual package and this amount will thicken 2 cups of liquid to make a solid. High acid foods or high sugar content foods can slow setting and reduce the thickening power. This can be a problem when using fresh lemon juice.

Tapioca Thickener (275)

Minute tapioca will make a clear thickener. It is good used in sauces or fruit fillings that are to be frozen. It is also good used in high-acid fruit sauces because it doesn't lose its thickening power. For a medium sauce, use 2 teaspoons per cup of liquid. For a thicker sauce use 1 tablespoon per cup. If tapioca is overcooked, it becomes stringy. Cook tapioca only to the boiling point, remove from heat, cool for 3 or 4 minutes, and stir. Wait a few more minutes and stir again. As it cools, it thickens.

Tomatoes (General Instructions) **(276)**

Which tomato to dry? Maturity of the fruit, soil conditions, moisture content and variety determine whether a tomato turns dark in dehydration. The Ace tomato has a low moisture content, and is one of the higher acid tomatoes available for planting in the home garden. The best way to know if tomatoes will turn dark is by drying a few. Occasionally one fruit will darken. Dark tomatoes are not harmful but they do not look appetizing and should be thrown away. All tomatoes are low on the acid scale but canning varieties have a higher acid content and a lower moisture content than other varieties. The soil helps determine the acid content of a tomato. The same tomato seed grown in two different locations will show a different acid content. If tomatoes are left on the vine after they are mature, a chemical change takes place that can cause the fruit to turn dark when it is dehydrated. Tests were made with low-acid yellow, pear, Ace and a cannery variety of tomatoes which also had a low moisture content and they all dried beautifully. From experiments used, the age (enzymatic browning) and the moisture content seemed to be the determining factor in good color retention. Choose a variety that grows well in the area in which you live. Check with the Extension Service in your county to determine which variety is low moisture and high acid. Be sure to dry them when they are in prime condition.

Tomato Barbecue Sauce (277)

- 2 cups lightly packed dehydrated tomatoes
- 2⅔ cups water
- ⅓ cup vinegar
- 1 Tbsp Worcestershire sauce
- 3 Tbsp lemon juice

Puree above ingredients in blender until smooth. Add:

- 1 Tbsp butter
- 1 Tbsp salad oil
- ½ Tbsp dehydrated onion
- 1 Tbsp flour
- 1 tsp prepared mustard
- ¼ cup firmly packed brown sugar
- ½ tsp salt

Puree in blender until well blended. Place in refrigerator in a tightly sealed container overnight. Good with all meats and poultry.

Tomato Butter (278)

- 2 Tbsp tomato puree
- 1 square margarine
- Dash white pepper
- ½ tsp seasoned salt

Make puree by placing ¼ cup tomato slices and ¼ cup boiling water in a blender. Let stand 5 minutes and then puree. Soften margarine but do not melt. Add margarine, pepper, and seasoned salt to the puree and chill.

Goes well with fish or sour dough bread.

Tomato-Cheese Rarebit (279)

- ¼ cup butter, melted
- 5 Tbsp flour
- 1 tsp salt
- ⅛ tsp pepper
- ½ tsp Worcestershire sauce
- 2 cups tomato sauce
- 1 cup grated sharp cheese

To make tomato juice, place 2 cups loosely packed dehydrated tomatoes in a blender, add water to the 2-cup measure, and puree.

Melt butter. Add flour, salt, pepper and Worcestershire sauce; blend thoroughly. Stir in tomato juice slowly. Cook, stirring constantly, until smooth and thick. Add cheese; heat just until cheese is melted, stirring occasionally. Serve on toast or muffins.

Low-Calorie Tomato Dressing (280)

- ⅓ cup dehydrated tomatoes reconstituted in 1 cup boiling water
- ¼ cup salad oil
- ¼ cup vinegar
- 1 tsp seasoned salt
- ½ tsp dry mustard
- ¼ tsp garlic salt
- ¼ tsp onion salt
- 2 tsp steak sauce

Combine all ingredients and blend thoroughly. Chill. Good on salad greens. Makes 1½ cups with 19 calories per tablespoon.

Tomato Paste (281)

- 2 cups dehydrated tomato slices
- 1 cup boiling water
- ¼ tsp salt

Reconstitute tomato slices in boiling water until smooth.

Tomato Sauce (282)

- 2 cups dehydrated tomato slices
- 2¼ cups boiling water
- 1½ Tbsp dehydrated carrot
- 1½ Tbsp dehydrated, chopped celery
- 2½ Tbsp dehydrated, chopped onions
- 1½ tsp basil
- ¼ tsp oregano
- Dash garlic powder
- ¼ tsp salt

Place tomato slices, carrot, celery and onion in blender and add boiling water. Let stand 5 minutes. Puree until smooth, add dry ingredients, and blend thoroughly. This is better if it stands overnight or at least a few hours so the spices flavor the vegetables.

Tomato Slices (283)

Serve dehydrated tomato slices with other vegetable chips for dipping. Especially good served with avocado, onion or alfalfa sprout dip.

Cream of Tomato Soup (284)

- 2 cups half-and-half
- 2 cups dehydrated tomatoes
- 1 Tbsp sugar (optional)
- 1 Tbsp dehydrated onion
- Dash of pepper
- Dash of garlic salt
- 1 tsp salt
- 1 Tbsp flour
- 2 Tbsp soft butter

Reconstitute the tomatoes by adding boiling water to the 2-cup measure; let stand 5 minutes and puree.

Heat the half-and-half in a pan. Put the remaining ingredients in the blender container. Cover and process until smooth. Remove feeder cap and slowly pour hot half-and-half into the mixture while processing. Reheat over low heat and serve. Makes 4 servings.

T-V Juice (285)

- 1 cup dehydrated tomato slices
- ⅛ tsp garlic salt
- 1 tsp dehydrated green peppers
- ¼ cup dehydrated carrots
- Few drops Tobasco Sauce
- 3 cups water
- ¼ cup dehydrated celery
- 1 Tbsp dehydrated onion
- ¼ tsp sugar (optional)
- ½ tsp salt

Place all ingredients, except Tobasco Sauce and salt, in a pan and simmer for 10 minutes. Cool for 5 minutes and puree in a blender until smooth. Press through a strainer to remove any pulp. Season with salt and a few drops of Tobasco Sauce. Chill and serve with a slice of fresh lemon. On a cold morning, this is also good served hot.

Save the pulp, add Italian Seasoning and use as paste to make a pizza.

Whipped Topping (286)

- 1 envelope unflavored gelatin
- 2 Tbsp cold water
- ¼ cup boiling water
- ⅔ cup water (room temperature)
- 1 cup instant nonfat dehydrated milk
- 2 Tbsp lemon juice
- ½ cup sugar
- 1 Tbsp Crisco oil
- ½ tsp lemon extract
- 1 tsp vanilla

Sprinkle gelatin over 2 tablespoons of cold water and let stand 3 minutes. Add boiling water and stir until the gelatin is completely dissolved. Cool to room temperature.

Place water and dry milk crystals in a large mixer bowl and whip until soft peaks form. It will take about 5 minutes. Then add lemon juice and continue whipping until stiff peaks form. Add sugar, oil, flavorings and gelatin mixture gradually, scraping sides of bowl until well mixed. Chill, and it is ready to use.

Tuna and Rice (Camper's Delight) (287)

- 2 7-oz cans dehydrated tuna
- 1⅓ cups minute brown rice (see recipes #238 or #240)
- 2 cups boiling water
- 2 Tbsp dehydrated onion
- 2 Tbsp dehydrated green peppers

Place all ingredients in a pan and bring to a boil. Cover and cook 10 to 15 minutes.

Turkey Cacciatore (288)

- 3 Tbsp margarine
- 1 cup diced green pepper
- ½ Tbsp dehydrated onion
- 1 clove garlic, minced
- 1½ Tbsp flour
- 2 cups dehydrated tomatoes
- 1 tsp salt
- 2 tsp Worcestershire sauce
- 3 cups dehydrated ground turkey reconstituted by steaming

Reconstitute tomatoes in 1 cup boiling water by chopping in the blender (do not puree).

In a medium saucepan, melt margarine. Add green pepper, dehydrated onion and garlic; saute until tender, about 5 minutes. Stir in flour; cook and stir for 1 minute. Blend in tomatoes, salt and Worcestershire sauce. Cook and stir until the mixture boils and thickens. Add turkey; mix well but gently. Simmer, covered, until turkey is hot, stirring occasionally, about 10 minutes. Serve over brown minute rice or toast. Serves 4.

Vanilla Wafers (289)

- ½ cup butter
- ½ cup shortening
- ⅔ cup granulated sugar
- 2 tsp vanilla
- 1 tsp salt
- 2 eggs
- 2¾ cups sifted flour

Cream butter, shortening and sugar. Add vanilla and salt. Add eggs, one at a time, beating well after each addition. Stir in flour, mixing well. Drop from a teaspoon 2 inches apart on a greased cookie sheet. Flatten with a floured, flat-bottom glass. Bake at 375° F. for 8 to 10 minutes. Makes 7 dozen cookies.

Orange-Glazed Wafers: While cookies are still hot, brush with ½ cup of sifted powdered sugar mixed with 1 tablespoon orange juice and ¼ teaspoon grated orange peel. Dot with bits of candied ginger.

Vanilla Wafer Crust (Microwave) (290)

- ¼ cup butter
- 1½ cups Vanilla Wafer crumbs (about 40 wafers)

Place butter in a 9-inch pie plate. Microwave on high for 30 seconds. Mix in Vanilla Wafer crumbs and press against the bottom and sides of the pie plate. Use an 8-inch glass pie plate to press the crumbs into a 9-inch plate. Microwave on medium, uncovered, for 3 minutes, rotate after 1 minute. Cool before filling.

The crust can be baked in a conventional oven at 375° F. for 8 minutes.

Walnuts (General Instructions) (291)

English walnut trees drop ripe walnuts over a one to two month time period. Pick up any nuts that have dropped and place a sheet under the tree. Shake the limbs vigorously to get all of the mature nuts. This process may have to be repeated for several weeks to complete the harvest. When the nuts are mature, the hulls crack and loosen. Remove the hulls that adhere to the nuts by hand. Dry the nuts the same day they are harvested to prevent deterioration. Place them on dehydrator trays and dry at 105° F. To test for dryness, allow a nut to cool. If the kernels and membranes are brittle and not soft and rubbery, they are dry.

Bleaching to lighten the shell color does not improve the quality in any way. Shells must be clean and the nuts must be thoroughly dry before bleaching. Sort the nuts and remove any split nuts because the bleach solution (entering the split) will ruin the flavor of the nutmeat. Do not use sulfur to bleach, as it will affect the nut flavor.

Dilute household bleach with about 4 to 6 parts of water to 1 part of bleach. Use a plastic bucket and work outside. Place the nuts in a wire basket, dip them into the solution, and stir them vigorously for 30 seconds. Do not leave the nuts in the bleaching solution more than 60 seconds. Lift the nuts out of the solution and rinse them quickly with water. Spread them one-layer deep on trays and place them in a well-ventilated room to air dry for 24 to 48 hours. Stir them occasionally until they are dry.

Properly stored nuts retain quality and flavor. Nuts stored in the shell have a shelf life of about 1 year. Bleached nuts only last about 6 months. Shelled nuts will only keep for 3 to 4 months under refrigeration, but if placed in the freezer they will be good for about a year. Freezer life is extended if they are vacuum sealed before placing them in the freezer.

Refer to the section on proper storage for foods.

Instant Wheat (General Instructions) (292)

By cooking wheat and drying it, it is possible to have precooked wheat with the advantage of more rapid preparation time. It only requires minutes instead of hours to serve wheat dishes.

Conventional Method

Place 2 cups of water in a covered saucepan; bring to a boil. Add 1 cup of wheat and steam until wheat is tender and all water is absorbed. This usually takes about 40 minutes. Spread the cooled, cooked wheat thinly on dehydrator trays and dry.

Microwave Method

Bring 1½ cups of water to a boil in a glass-covered casserole. Add ¾ cup of wheat and cook on simmer for 25 minutes or until all moisture is absorbed and the wheat is tender. Let stand covered for 5 minutes. Place on dehydrator trays and dry. *Caution:* If cooked on high, the kernels burst.

Instant Wheat Cereal (Microwave) (293)

½ cup wheat (whole kernels)
1 Tbsp water
Dash of salt

Place in a cereal bowl. Rub the top of the bowl with butter to prevent boil over. Cook on reheat for 2 minutes, or until hot. Serve with fresh fruits and cream.

Wheat Snack Cracker (294)

- 1½ cups water
- ⅓ cup peanut oil
- 2 Tbsp honey
- 1½ cups instant wheat ground into flour

Place water, oil and honey in a blender and mix. Add flour gradually until mixture is thick and holds together. Remove from the blender and spread on a teflex sheet or solid sheet, score in 1-inch pieces and dry in dehydrator until crisp. Set dehydrator at 145° F.

Instant Wheat Salad (295)

- 2 cups water
- 1 cup instant wheat
- 1 Armenian cucumber
- 2 fresh tomatoes
- 1 green bell pepper
- ½ cup fresh parsley, chopped
- 1 bunch small green onions
- 4 Tbsp lemon juice
- ¼ cup olive oil
- ½ cup drained garbanzos
- Salt and pepper to taste

Put the water into a saucepan and bring it to a boil; slowly add the instant wheat. Place a lid on the pan and simmer 10 minutes or until the wheat absorbs the water. Set aside to cool. Wash cucumber and dice. Wash tomatoes and slice into small cubes. Wash and cube bell pepper. Wash and chop fresh parsley. Wash and finely slice green onions using tender stems also. Mix lemon juice and olive oil. Drain garbanzos. In a large salad bowl, combine cooled wheat and vegetables. Toss lightly, add lemon juice and oil dressing. Serve on a bed of alfalfa sprouts, or mix 1 cup sprouts into salad and serve in Pita Pockets.

Bulgur Wheat (General Instructions) (296)

Bulgur is a precooked, dried, cracked wheat. It is toasted in appearance, has a nutty flavor, and can be used in many dishes. Follow the instant wheat recipe and when the wheat is thoroughly dry, remove the outer bran layer by rubbing the kernels between hands. It may be necessary to moisten either hands or wheat surface to assist in the removal of the chaff. Crack the wheat in a mill, grinder or blender. For highest nutritional value, crack only as needed. Cooked wheat is soft enough to be cracked in a blender without damaging the blender.

When recipes call for cooked bulgur, boil in water for five minutes. Bulgur, when cooked, will double in volume.

Bulgur Pilaf (Wheat) (297)

- 1 cup bulgur
- ½ Tbsp dehydrated onion
- 2 Tbsp butter
- 2 cups chicken broth
- ½ tsp oregano
- ½ cup dehydrated mushrooms

Saute bulgur and onion in butter until the pilaf is golden and the onion is softened. Stir in broth, seasoning, and mushrooms. Cover. Bake at 350° F. for 30 minutes. Serves 4. Pilaf may also be made by bringing the bulgur to a boil, reducing the heat, and simmering for 10 minutes.

Bulgur-Vermicelli Pilaf (Wheat) (298)

- 1 coil vermicelli
- 2 cups water or broth
- Salt and pepper
- 1 cube butter
- 1 cup coarsely-ground bulgur

Brown vermicelli in ¾ cube butter; add liquid, bring to a boil. Add bulgur, salt and pepper. Simmer until liquid is absorbed, approximately 20 minutes. Add remaining butter and mix well. Serves 4.

Won-Ton Skins (299)

- 2¼ cups plain flour
- ½ tsp salt
- ½ cup boiling water
- ¼ cup vegetable oil

Sift flour and salt into a bowl. Slowly stir in boiling water. Blend until smooth. Cover the bowl, let stand 30 minutes. Place dough on a well-oiled board and knead with hands and fingers that have been rubbed with oil. Knead until the dough becomes bouncy and elastic. Roll into 3 ropes, 1-inch in diameter. Wrap each rope in wax paper except the one to be cut. Cut off ¼-inch disks and roll as thin as possible (square or round). Stack and keep covered while rolling the other ropes. Dust with cornstarch to prevent them from sticking to each other. Place 1½ teaspoons stuffing in the center and seal. They may be served in soups, like stuffed dumplings, or they may be deep-fried wth fruit or meat fillings.

Fried Fruit Pies (300)

Use fruit butters or pie fillings to fill skins.

Place 1 teaspoon of fruit filling in a 3 × 3-inch skin. Fold two corners to the center and moisten with water and place the other two corners over the first two so they will hold the fruit in the center. Deep-fat fry at 350° F., a few at a time, until browned. Serve warm, sprinkled with powdered sugar.

Yam-Orange Pudding (301)

- 1 cup dehydrated yams
- 5 eggs
- ½ tsp salt
- 1 cup milk
- ½ cup sugar
- 1 cup fresh orange juice

Reconstitute dehydrated yams by placing in a blender and adding boiling water to the 1-cup measure. Let stand 5 minutes and blend until smooth.

In a large bowl mix together yams and remaining ingredients. Turn into a greased 8 × 8 × 2-inch baking dish or six 6-ounce custard cups. Place in larger pan filled with 1 inch of water. Bake at 350° F. for 1 hour and 15 minutes for baking dish, or 45 minutes for cups, until the tip of a knife inserted near the center comes out clean. Serve warm with whipped cream. Serves 6.

Yam-Pineapple Bake (302)

- 4 cups dehydrated yams
- 1 cup pineapple tidbits with syrup
- 3 Tbsp softened butter
- 1 tsp salt
- 2 cups miniature marshmallows
- ¼ cup pecan halves

Place dehydrated yams in a blender and add water to the 4-cup measure. Puree until reconstituted and smooth. Mix pineapple, butter and salt together. Add reconstituted yams. Place half of the mixture in a 2-quart casserole and top with 1 cup miniature marshmallows. Add remaining yams. Decorate with pecan halves. Cover and bake at 350° F. for 20 minutes. Uncover and place 1 cup of miniature marshmallows over the top. Bake 10 minutes more, or until the marshmallows are toasty brown. Serves 6.

Note: Reduce the temperature 25 degrees for glass containers when baking.

Yogurt (303)

- 1 Tbsp unflavored gelatin
- ¼ cup cold water
- 2 cups low-fat fluid milk
- ⅔ cup instant nonfat powdered milk
- ⅓ cup yogurt

Sprinkle gelatin over ¼-cup cold water and let stand for 3 minutes. Pour the milk into a pan and heat to 180° F.; or, if using the microwave, place milk in a 2-quart measuring cup and heat at full power, using the probe. Temperatures are important when making yogurt. Remove the milk from the stove and pour into a 2-quart measuring cup. Add the dissolved gelatin and the powdered milk. Mix thoroughly with a fork or a wire whisk. Add warm water to the 1-quart measure. Check the temperature. When it reaches 120° F., take one or two tablespoons of the warm milk and mix it into the yogurt start to make a thin, smooth mixture. Pour the yogurt starter back into the milk mixture and mix until smooth. Pour into individual 1-cup containers, cover and place in dehydrator set at 115° F. to coagulate. The milk should reach a custardy consistency in about 3 to 6 hours. For a sharper flavor, lengthen the incubation time. If the dehydrator is equipped with recirculating air, close the vent. This makes 1 quart. Be sure to reserve ⅓ cup plain yogurt to be used as a start. Refrigerate the yogurt until it is used. It should keep for a week, if held at normal refrigerator temperature.

Yogurt Leather (303A)

Yogurt leathers are delicious and nutritious. Use a flavored yogurt. Spread it onto a teflex sheet and dry the same as fruit leather. Use about 2 cups per tray. It is good for snacking and backpacking.

Yogurt Drops (303B)

Use commercially-flavored yogurt or refer to recipes for making flavored yogurt. Drop quarter teaspoonfuls onto sheets to dry. They make very good bite-sized snacks.

Frozen Yogurt Pie (304)

Make 2 deep-dish graham cracker pie crusts.

Blend 1 pint of strawberry yogurt with a 9-ounce container of whipped topping (see recipe #286). Put in a shell and place in the freezer for 4 hours. One-half hour before serving, move the pie to the refrigerator. Top with fresh fruit slices if desired.

Try combining a lemon and a blueberry yogurt, with fresh blueberries as a garnish. Many tempting flavors may be used.

Yogurt Chicken Curry (Microwave Method) (305)

- 2 whole chicken breasts
- ½ cup water
- 2 Tbsp cornstarch
- 2 Tbsp butter
- 1 Tbsp dehydrated onions
- 1 tsp curry powder
- ¾ tsp chili powder
- ¾ tsp cinnamon
- ½ tsp salt
- 1 bay leaf, crumbled
- ¼ cup dehydrated coconut
- 1 cup plain yogurt

Halve, skin and bone the chicken breasts. Cut the chicken into ¾-inch cubes. Combine water, cornstarch, butter and onion in a 1½-quart microwave glass baking dish with lid. Cover and cook on high in microwave 2 minutes, stirring once. Add chicken, curry powder, chili powder, cinnamon, salt and bay leaf. Cover and cook 4 minutes longer, stirring twice. Stir in coconut and yogurt. Serve with rice and a condiment plate of sliced fruit, peanuts, monukka raisins and steamed julienne green beans. Serves 4.

Yogurt Chicken Curry (Conventional Method) **(306)**

- 2 whole chicken breasts
- ¼ cup water
- 2 Tbsp cornstarch
- 1 tsp curry powder
- ½ tsp chili powder
- ½ tsp cinnamon
- ½ tsp salt
- 1 bay leaf, crumbled
- 2 Tbsp butter
- 1 Tbsp dehydrated onion
- ¼ cup dehydrated coconut
- 1 cup plain yogurt

Halve, skin and bone the chicken breasts. Cut the chicken into ¾-inch cubes. Mix 2 tablespoons water with cornstarch, curry powder, chili powder, cinnamon, salt and bay leaf. Add chicken and toss to coat. Saute chicken in butter 3 minutes. Add onion, coconut and remaining 2 tablespoons of water. Cook 3 to 5 minutes longer, or until the chicken is tender. Stir in yogurt. Serve with rice and a condiment plate of sliced fruit, peanuts, monukka raisins and steamed julienne green beans. Serves 4.

Five-Alive Yogurt (307)

- 1½ Tbsp frozen five-alive juice concentrate
- ¼ tsp unflavored gelatin
- 1 Tbsp sugar
- 1 drop orange food coloring
- ¾ cup basic yogurt mix (see recipe #303)

Measure the juice concentrate into a glass measure. Sprinkle unflavored gelatin over the juice until it is absorbed. Add sugar, orange food coloring and mix well. Place in microwave oven on high for 1 minute. Pour into bottom of yogurt container, and add yogurt; mix. Place a lid on container and put in dehydrator at 115° F. until set. Stir before placing in refrigerator and again after, if necessary.

Yogurt Fruit Sauce (308)

- 1 cup vanilla yogurt
- 2 Tbsp orange-cranberry relish

Mix well and use as a dressing over a fruit salad or as a dip for fresh fruit slices.

Lemon Yogurt (309)

- 1 Tbsp sugar
- ¼ tsp lemon extract
- ¼ tsp tumeric color*
- ¾ cup basic yogurt mix (see recipe #303)

Place sugar, lemon extract and tumeric color in the bottom of a one-cup container. Add yogurt mix and stir well. Place lid on container and place in a dehydrator at 115° F. until set. It could take from 3 to 6 hours. When yogurt is set, place in refrigerator to cool. Stir again before using.

Tumeric Color

Place ¼ teaspoon of ground tumeric into ¼ cup of water and bring to a boil. Simmer for 2 minutes; cool. This procedure allows the volatile oils to dissipate and it can then be used as a natural yellow food color.

Pineapple Yogurt (310)

- 3 Tbsp cooked, crushed pineapple
- 1 Tbsp sugar
- ¼ tsp pineapple extract
- ¾ cup basic yogurt mix (see recipe #303)

Measure 3 tablespoons cooked crushed pineapple into a one-cup container. Add 1 tablespoon sugar and ¼ teaspoon pineapple extract. Add yogurt mix. Place a lid on the container and place it in the dehydrator at 115° F. until set. Stir before putting in refrigerator and again before serving.

Vanilla Yogurt (311)

- ½ tsp vanilla extract
- 1 Tbsp brown sugar
- ¾ cup basic yogurt mix (see recipe #303)

Place vanilla extract and brown sugar in the bottom of a yogurt container. Add yogurt mix. Place a lid on the container and place it in the dehydrator at 115° F. until set. Stir before putting in refrigerator and again before serving.

Orange Yogurt (312)

- 1½ Tbsp frozen orange juice concentrate
- ¼ tsp unflavored gelatin
- 1 Tbsp sugar
- ¾ cup basic yogurt mix (see recipe #303)

Measure orange juice concentrate into a glass measure. Sprinkle unflavored gelatin over juice and let it stand for 3 minutes. Add sugar, mix well, and place in a microwave oven on high for 1 minute. Pour into the bottom of the yogurt container, and add yogurt mix. Place a lid on the container and put it in the dehydrator at 115° F. until set. Stir before placing in refrigerator and again after, if necessary.

Lime Yogurt (313)

- 1½ Tbsp frozen lime juice concentrate
- ¼ tsp unflavored gelatin
- 1 Tbsp sugar
- 1 drop green food coloring
- ¾ cup basic yogurt mix (see recipe #303)

Measure frozen lime juice concentrate into a glass measure. Sprinkle unflavored gelatin over the juice until it is absorbed. Add sugar, green food coloring, and mix well. Place in a microwave oven on high for 1 minute. Pour into bottom of yogurt container, and add yogurt mix. Place a lid on the container and put it in the dehydrator at 115° F. until set. Stir before placing in the refrigerator and again after, if necessary.

Yogurt Strawberry Pie (314)

- 1 envelope unflavored gelatin
- 1 cup cold milk, divided in half
- ½ cup sugar
- ¼ tsp salt
- 1 cup cottage cheese
- 2 cups strawberry flavored yogurt
- ¼ tsp almond extract
- 1 9-inch graham cracker crust

Mix gelatin with ½ cup milk; let stand 1 minute. Stir over medium heat until the gelatin is completely dissolved. Add sugar, salt and remaining ½ cup milk; stir until sugar is dissolved. Chill until slightly thickened. Place cottage cheese in a blender and puree until very smooth. Beat in yogurt and almond extract. Stir in thickened gelatin. Pour into crumb crust. Chill 4 hours, or until firm.

Yogurt Pastry Shell (315)

- ¾ cup flour
- ¼ tsp salt
- 4 Tbsp shortening
- 4 Tbsp plain yogurt

Stir flour and salt together; cut in shortening. Add yogurt. Gently stir until moistened. Form into a ball and flatten on a lightly-floured surface. Roll 1/8-inch thick. Place the pastry into a 9-inch pie plate. Prick with fork and flute edges. Bake at 450° F. about 10 minutes.

Yogurt Pops (316)

- 1 cup plain yogurt
- 1 6-oz can water
- 1 6-oz can frozen concentrated juice

Combine ingredients and mix until smooth. Pour into 4-ounce plastic cups or pop molds. When partially frozen, insert a wooden stick in each to be used as a handle. Freeze until firm. Makes 6.

Spiced apple yogurt goes well with apple juice. Plain yogurt with orange juice makes a creamsicle. Let the kids take over. With their imagination this could prove to be very interesting.

Yogurt Set Salad (317)

- ½ cup water
- 1 3-oz pkg lemon gelatin
- ½ cup milk
- 2 cups plain yogurt
- 2 Tbsp lemon juice
- ½ cup diced cucumber, unpared
- ½ cup diced carrot
- 2 Tbsp minced onion
- 2 Tbsp minced parsley
- Salad greens
- Monterey Jack cheese
- Cucumber twists
- Carrot curls
- Radish roses

Heat water to boiling. Add gelatin and stir over low heat until dissolved. Cool. Stir in milk, yogurt and lemon juice, mixing with wire whip until smooth. Chill until it begins to thicken (it may take only a few minutes). Fold in cucumber, carrot, onion and parsley. Pour into a 4-cup salad mold. Chill until firm.

Invert onto plate. Garnish with greens, cheese, and vegetables.

Yogurt Stroganoff (318)

- 1½ lbs lean beef
- 3 Tbsp flour
- 1 tsp salt
- ⅛ tsp pepper
- 2 Tbsp butter
- 1½ Tbsp dehydrated onion
- 1 cup water
- 3 Tbsp catsup
- 1 tsp Worcestershire sauce
- ½ tsp garlic powder
- 1 cup plain yogurt
- ½ cup dehydrated mushroom stems and pieces rehydrated

Cut beef into 1-inch cubes. Roll beef in flour mixed with salt and pepper. Brown beef in butter a few pieces at a time over medium-high heat. Return all beef to skillet, add liquid drained from reconstituting mushrooms, onions, water, catsup, Worcestershire sauce and garlic powder. Do not stir, but cover and bring to a boil. Reduce heat and simmer, stirring occasionally about 1 hour, or until tender and sauce is thickened. Just before serving, stir yogurt until smooth and add with mushrooms to the beef. Heat 1 or 2 minutes. Serve over brown rice.

Yogurt Vegetable Salad (319)

- 1½ cups plain yogurt
- 1 cup finely-chopped raw vegetables
- 1 tsp finely-minced fresh ginger
- Dash cayenne
- Dash curry powder

Choose two or more vegetables (such as radishes, cucumber, green pepper, green onions, tomatoes) and stir into yogurt. Season with fresh ginger, cayenne and curry powder. Serve on a bed of lettuce or salad greens with slices of longhorn cheese and wheat crackers.

Zucchini Cake (Mock Pumpkin) (320)

- 3 cups dehydrated grated zucchini
- 2 cups boiling water
- 4 eggs, slightly beaten
- 1¼ cups sugar
- 2 cups evaporated milk
- ¾ tsp salt
- 3 tsp pumpkin pie spice
- 1 yellow cake mix (dry)
- 1 cube margarine
- 1 cup chopped nuts

Puree zucchini and water to make 3½ cups total. (It may be necessary to add a little more water to equal the 3½ cups.) In a large mixer bowl, slightly beat eggs and blend sugar into eggs. Add milk, zucchini, salt and spice. Mix as for pie. Pour into a greased 9 x 13-inch pan. Sprinkle dry cake mix over the top. Melt margarine and drizzle over top of cake mix. Sprinkle with chopped nuts. Bake at 350° F. for 80 minutes. Cool slightly and serve with whipped cream. It is also good cold with ice cream.

This recipe may be used with dehydrated pumpkin also.

Zucchini Pie (Mock Pumpkin) (321)

- 2 cups dehydrated zucchini, grated
- ½ tsp salt
- ¼ tsp cloves
- 1 cup milk
- 2 eggs
- 1 9-inch unbaked pastry shell
- ½ tsp mace
- ½ tsp ginger
- 1 cup sugar
- ½ cup evaporated milk

Use the yellow variety of zucchini and peel the squash before grating and drying. Reconstitute grated zucchini by placing 2 cups in a blender container and adding boiling water to the two-cup measure. Puree until smooth. Add remaining ingredients and pour into an unbaked pastry shell. Bake at 450° F. for 10 minutes, then reduce the heat to 325° F. for 40 minutes, or until done.

This recipe may be used with dehydrated pumpkin also.

Zucchini Yeast Rolls (322)

- ½ cup dehydrated zucchini
- ¼ cup sugar
- ¼ cup shortening
- ½ tsp salt
- ½ cup scalded milk
- ½ cake compressed yeast
- ¼ cup lukewarm water
- 2½ cups flour

Reconstitute zucchini in ½ cup boiling water and puree to make ½ cup. Combine zucchini, sugar, shortening and salt with milk; heat to lukewarm. Dissolve yeast in water and add to milk mixture. Add flour and mix well. Dough will be soft. Let rise until doubled. Knead and shape into pan rolls and let rise again until doubled. Bake at 400° F. for 15 to 20 minutes.

Chocolate Zucchini Cake (323)

- 2½ cups flour
- 2½ tsp baking powder
- 1½ tsp soda
- 1 tsp salt
- 1 tsp cinnamon
- ½ cup cocoa
- ¾ cup margarine
- 2 cups sugar
- 3 eggs
- 2 tsp orange peel
- 2 tsp vanilla
- 2 cups lightly-packed zucchini
- ½ cup milk
- 1 cup nuts (optional)

Reconstitute zucchini by adding water to the 2-cup measure and blend until smooth.

Combine dry ingredients. Beat together margarine and sugar; add eggs one at a time. Add orange peel, vanilla, water and zucchini. Alternately stir in dry ingredients and milk. Add nuts last. Pour into a greased and floured 10-inch tube or bundt pan. Bake at 350° F. for 1 hour or until done. Cool in pan 15 minutes. Drizzle glaze* over cake.

*Glaze

- 2 cups powdered sugar
- 3 Tbsp milk
- 1 tsp vanilla

Mix well and glaze cake.

Candied Zucchini (324)

- 12 firm medium-size zucchini, peeled
- 4 cups sugar
- 1½ cups water
- 2 Tbsp lemon juice, strained

Cut the zucchini in ½-inch cubes. Make a syrup by boiling sugar and water for 5 minutes. Drop the zucchini cubes into the syrup and cook until just barely tender. Stir in the lemon juice. Marinate in the syrup for 12 hours. Drain and place on teflex sheets to dry. Set dehydrator at 120° F.

Use in place of candied fruit peels.

Zucchini Pineapple Drops (325)

- 2 lrg zucchini, peeled & seeded
- 1 46-oz can unsweetened pineapple juice
- 1½ cups lemon juice
- Yellow food coloring
- 3 cups sugar

Grate zucchini coarsely to make 1 gallon. Use extra-large zucchini because it has more meat and is whiter. Add pineapple juice, lemon juice, enough food coloring to make a light yellow color, and sugar. Simmer 20 minutes. This makes approximately 6 one-quart containers. It can be dried as fruit leather or snack drops. It can also be frozen for drying at a later time. To make fruit roll, pour two cups of mixture on a teflex sheet to dry. To make snack drops, drop by the teaspoonful on a teflex sheet to dry. It takes approximately 12 hours to dry. To reconstitute, add ½ cup water to a roll of broken leather pieces and let it stand for 30 minutes. Stir occasionally, so that all pieces of the leather reconstitute equally. It can be used for cottage cheese/pineapple salad, or substituted in any recipe calling for crushed pineapple. When using it for a gelatin salad, just add an additional ¼ cup boiling water to the gelatin and let the leather reconstitute as the salad sets.

Index

(This book is indexed by recipe numbers.)

J

L

M

R

S

T

V